Focus on the Future

Re-Entry Journal & Workbook

By:

SWOP

BEHIND BARS

(With some content by Bob Pelshaw and others)

340 South Lemon Street
Walnut, CA 91789

swopbehindbars@gmail.com

ISBN: 1985307405
ISBN-13: 978-1985307407

DEDICATION

This guide is dedicated to those who have explored commercialized sexual services, consensually or by coercion, and are without a voice to help navigate through the challenges that they and their families face because of - though not limited to: criminalization, discrimination, stigma, substance use and abuse, and incarceration. We strive to reconnect individuals and families through holistic and integral re/entry support services.

We've been there.

We are here.

We care.

CONTENTS

CHAPTER 1
Getting Started

I remember my first day in prison—one of the hardest days of my life. Nothing up to that point had prepared me for incarceration. The second hardest day of my life was the day I was released from prison. I was even less prepared for life once I got out.

If you've spent time in jail or prison, you quickly realize everyone has their own way to "do time." Some people read, sleep all day, play cards, workout, or focus on whatever they can to keep their minds busy. Many people immerse themselves in programming if their facility offers it. Even if offered, it doesn't mean the material will be useful.

As a business owner I was impressed with the entrepreneurial talent most of my fellow-incarcerated citizens had. Everyone had a "hustle" inside prison; myself included. One of mine was to help people write business plans and resumes. Most of the fellas I served time with dreamed of starting their own *legal* businesses. Many of them had vast business experience running illegal businesses; mostly in illegal drugs. I looked around for material to help them, and finding nothing, I wrote my own. Thankfully ***Illegal to Legal: Business Success for the (Formerly) Incarcerated*** has since become the number one tool nationally for teaching the incarcerated and formerly incarcerated entrepreneurial skills. The book, workbook, and course can show how to take your street skills and life experience and use them to make a legitimate income, whether from employment, business, or both.

Our society celebrates entrepreneurialism – that "hustle" that lets people achieve the American dream. Good 'ole American work ethic and American ingenuity seem ingrained in the cultural fabric of our nation. I've always said that if you know what to do to start and operate it a drug business, you have the skills to run a thriving business that is legal. The same holds true for sex workers.

I understand why our society shuns those that have used their business skills, ingenuity, and work ethic in ways contrary to our current laws and standards. Before my own incarceration, I was one of the judgmental employers that refused to hire someone with a criminal history, even though every one of us break laws daily. After prison I had to learn to overcome and move past the shame of being a felon: the very type of person I mistakenly had thought I was better than.

At the time of the publication of this workbook there has been a lot of public attention on the #MeToo movement and powerful men in Hollywood, the business community, and elsewhere that have sexually abused woman. This helped usher in conversations about equal pay for women. That attention is long overdue. Deeper conversations, and proactive changes, are needed on these and more issues affecting women and society as a whole.

Everyone deserves respect and dignity. Many people do things to survive that society, our families, and sometimes the law, may not approve of. I wrote *Illegal to Legal* to help give all people alternatives. Everyone deserves a second chance. Sadly, not everyone is ready for their second chance.

I am honored to partner with the Sex Workers Outreach Project (SWOP) and SWOP Behind Bars to provide this much-needed manual as a resource to help incarcerated women and sex workers prepare to be ready for their second chance. The team from SWOP provided the concept and most of this material. I mostly worked on chapters 1-3, much of which are excerpts from *Illegal to Legal*.

This Guide is designed to give practical steps to prepare for reentry. Along the way it also will provide guidance and inspiration to help you create a new life. There's even places where you can begin to journal about your personal journey and learn to use journaling as an avenue for healing. Use this Guide as a tool, frequently. It's written by people who have been where you are and have used the skills taught in this Guide to thrive after prison or jail.

In this Guide we try to give you an overview of the main things you'll need to create a solid foundation for your new life, but it's not everything you need. Keep searching, learning, trying, and making the right decisions.

Most importantly, try to get involved with a group of positive people to share our journey; whether a church, an Alcoholics Anonymous (AA), Narcotics Anonymous (NA), or Substance Abuse (SA) group, or whatever you choose to connect with.

I've learned that if you've survived prison, you can survive, and do, anything! I believe even more so if you've been a sex worker. For those of you who may not know, a sex worker is someone who exchanges sexual services for money or other gain.

Don't let your past define you. You have a bright future ahead, which you must fight every day to create. Use this Guide as a resource to help give you the tools needed to succeed in your new life. You can do it. We believe in you!

- Bob Pelshaw, February 2018

CHAPTER 2
What To Do Before You're Released

It's never too early to start reentry preparation. Reentry can be a complicated process, but you are not alone on this journey. Re-launching life in the free world may be one of the toughest things you have ever done, but you can do it if you're willing to invest your time and effort in the process. We've been where you are now, and we want you to remember three things:

1. You are not alone in this quest, but it is up to you to create and follow a path, which this workbook helps you do.
2. Having and following a plan, and connecting with healthy people and situations, will increase your chances of successful reentry.
3. Others have made it, and so can you!

Reentering your community can be more manageable when you're aware of the services and resources available to help.

This workbook is designed to provide specific information to help answer questions and give you the tools needed to succeed on the outside. Here are the steps you should follow:

1. Contact the resource organizations listed, and when you do, make sure you are prepared with questions ready whenever possible.
2. Review your plan with your Case Manager, Bureau Social Worker, or Reentry Affairs Coordinator.

3. Get their input, ask questions, and see if they have any suggestions for you or any other areas where they can refer you to help and resources.

Using these resources has helped many succeed in finding work, supporting themselves and their families, and more. We want you to achieve the same.

You are a member of your community, and we want to help you transition home and succeed. ***When you succeed we all succeed.*** If you have any questions, don't hesitate to call us. Our contact information is at the end of this workbook.

Why do I need a plan?

The world-famous UCLA basketball coach John Wooden, winner of 11 national titles, said it best:

Failing to Plan is planning to fail.

Author and motivational teacher John Maxwell says, "ten minutes of planning saves two hours of work." Have you ever gone on vacation without a plan? What would a house look like if it was built without a plan? The best things need a plan to build them. You're one of those "best things!"

Plans aren't perfect, and the goal isn't to make a perfect plan. The goal is to help you make a plan to prepare for the success you can have in your post-release life. Your plan will change over time, but it's much better to have a plan that you can adjust than having no plan at all!

Maybe you've never made a plan for your life before, and that's OK. This workbook shows you how to plan in an easy and meaningful way. If you don't know what you should plan for, make a plan for what you should be doing, and don't be afraid to plan for your dreams. Your dreams will give you direction: the right one!

There are two types of plans this Workbook can help with:

1. A pre-release plan.
2. A post release plan.

Pre-release planning

Pre-release planning is the process to prepare you to transition from the institutional setting to the community. This plan is important whether you have been incarcerated a short or a long time because all groups face the same challenges regardless of the time served in your sentence.

Pre-release planning should begin a minimum of 90 days prior to projected release, if possible, but it is never too soon (or too late!) to start the process. If you don't have 90 days, you should still do what you can. Use the information in this workbook to guide you, and the checklists as a tool to help you navigate through all the things you need to do to build a foundation for a new future.

Start by making a plan for every week before your release. Write down your goals for that week and celebrate each accomplishment you make in your journey! Making a Daily Positive Vibe is a tool to help you realize you are more powerful than you think, you have more going for you than you think, and no matter what, you are worth the effort to make a you that lives and thrives on the outside!

Don't just plan your life outside of prison. Like my friend, and formerly incarcerated citizen Myron Pierce says, he "made a schedule within his prison schedule." Don't just do your time by wasting the opportunity to learn new habits and prepare for your new life. Schedule your days inside to make the most of your time. Set small goals for every day, and schedule time to work on those. There is more on effective goal setting and achievement in Chapter 7. Practice what you can from this Guide inside so you are ready to succeed where you are outside.

Post-release planning

Post-release planning gives you the tools you need to achieve your dream and live a new life. Why wait until you're out to deal with post-release issues? You can use your time while incarcerated to help build healthy habits to strengthen you and build a new future.

The rest of this chapter are checklists to help you jump start and manage your pre-release planning.

CHECKLIST #1: GET YOUR ID DOCUMENTS TOGETHER

TIMELINE: Start this at least 8 weeks before you leave, or as soon as you can, as quickly as you can.

- ☐ If you don't already have them, get your identification documents. Talk with your Case Manager or Reentry Affairs Coordinator about these documents because they can help you order a birth certificate.

- ☐ You can get a social security card or a replacement card for free from the Social Security Administration. If you do not get your card before you leave prison, the application and other information is included with your release paperwork (provided by SBB) 30 days before you leave prison.

- ☐ Birth certificates can be ordered while you are in prison from the state where you were born. If you do not get your birth certificate before you leave prison, this website shows you where to write to obtain vital records for each state and territory:

Birth Certificates may also be ordered online through http://www.vitalchek.com from any county health department in the US and sent by Express Mail to any address. All documents will arrive in 7 days or less if ordered with overnight delivery. The cost is approximately $35.00. You MUST be present to answer any security questions while filling out the online form. Your SBB case manager can help you do this if you are unable to access it while in prison.

Identification for Release
You should start to work towards getting these documents before you're released.

　　　_____*Birth Certificate*
　　　_____*Driver's License or State ID*
　　　_____*Social Security Card*

If you haven't already, make a folder, or a large envelope, where you can keep your documents and important papers organized.

CHECKLIST #2: THE REST OF YOUR RECORDS & ACCOMLISHMENTS

❑ Find out about any outstanding fees, fines, debts, or warrants.

❑ Speak to your Case Manager about how to find out if you have any outstanding fees, fines, warrants or debts. These can limit your ability to obtain employment, housing, or even lead to re-arrest.

❑ If you have outstanding child support payments, failing to manage this situation before your release could prevent you from getting a driver's license.

❑ Are you a veteran? If yes, make sure you have your military discharge papers. You can do obtain these either online (after your release) or by mail. If you choose to do by mail, check with your Case Manager to see if they can give you the paper form.

❑ Get proof of your GED / high school completion or any other classes you took while in prison.

❑ If you got your GED while in prison, make sure you have your transcript before you are released.

❑ Create a folder with everything positive you have done while in prison, including certificates for vocational training, drug treatment, anger management or any other cognitive behavioral therapy.

❑ Get your medical records. Ask Health Services about getting copies of your medical records while you are still in prison to help you transition to treatment in the community.

❑ Confirm your housing. Your Reentry Affairs Coordinator, Case Manager, or Social Worker (if available) can provide you information about finding a place to live in your release city. Social Workers can also help if you need special housing such as a nursing home, assisted living, senior housing, or group home placement.

Mental Health Services.
Adjusting to life outside of prison can be difficult at times; you may find yourself feeling discouraged or depressed. Many people – millions of Americans, in fact – experience mental health challenges, whether it is depression, anxiety, or some form of addiction. You should feel

comfortable asking any questions you have about your mental health with your primary care provider – and know that checkups and services are covered by most insurance companies as any other health service.

You can find free or low-cost mental health services available in your area on the Substance Abuse and Mental Health Services Administration (SAMHSA) website: https:// findtreatment.samhsa.gov/ or by calling the National Helpline 1-800-662-HELP/4357 (TDD: 1-800-487-4889). No matter what problems you are dealing with, there is a reason to keep on living. By calling 1-800-273-TALK (8255) at any time, you will be connected to a counselor at a crisis center in your area. You can also visit the National Suicide Prevention Lifeline website at: www.suicidepreventionlifeline.org.

Building Your Skills.

Having an education is important because it increases employment options. There are many ways to further your education upon release. Adult Basic Education (ABE) programs are for individuals who want to improve in reading, writing, math, listening, and speaking. ABE programs are offered at adult schools, career centers, libraries, or community colleges for free or for a small fee.

If you do not have a high school diploma or GED, you should enroll in a GED program as soon as possible after release. The GED test allows adults who have not completed high school to show they have the knowledge and skills associated with a high school diploma. Many community colleges offer programs that allow you to earn a GED and college credits at the same time. You can find GED test preparation classes near you at: www.gedtestingservice.com/testers/Locate-a-prep-center or by calling the toll-free number 1-800-MY-GED (1-800-626-9433).

If you have a high school diploma or GED and want to further your education, there are resources available to help you with the cost of college. Community colleges are a common option for individuals returning home from prison. The low cost of tuition and the variety of programs offered make these colleges an ideal starting place. By enrolling in a community college, you can earn an Associate's degree and then transfer to a four-year college or university to earn a Bachelor's degree.

The Free Application for Federal Student Aid (FAFSA) is the starting point for accessing all federal student financial aid. You can find FAFSA online at: http://www.fafsa.gov or you can request a paper copy from 1-

800-4-FED-AID (1-800-433-3243). Federal student aid information can be found at: http://www.StudentLoans.gov .

Vocational programs provide you with skills required for a job. They are also referred to as occupational, vo-tech, or career and technical education programs. Vocational programs are available through community and technical colleges, as well as trade schools, and they take less time to complete than academic college degree programs. You can apply at the local employment office, as a "displaced worker," for Department of Labor Second Chance Act funds if you want to learn a vocational trade.

Criminal record-based employment discrimination.
Under laws enforced by federal and/or state agencies employers must not treat anyone, including people with criminal records, differently based on their race, national origin, or another reason protected by law.

Voting and Weapons.
Find out if you have the right to vote in your state and if there is anything you need to do to restore your right to vote. Check with your local voting office to find out your rights. If you can do so, register to vote.

Anyone convicted of a felony is prohibited from possessing firearms or ammunition. In addition to physically holding or having a firearm or ammunition on you, "possession" also includes a firearm or ammunition that you have knowledge of, and control over, in an automobile or a home. Possession of a firearm or ammunition can result in new federal charges. Some states have also enacted additional restrictions on weapons such as tasers, stun guns, and crossbows. You should check with your probation officer or local law enforcement agency before you come into possession of any type of weapon.

CHECKLIST #3 - FIRST THINGS TO DO ON RELEASE

Do these in your first week of reentry. If you are transitioning through a Residential Reentry Center (RRC), staff at the center will be able to assist you with some of the items on this checklist. Find somewhere to access the internet. Most public libraries offer free internet access (although photo identification may be required) and library staff can help you. Most RRCs also have internet services.

1. **Get a State Issued photo ID**. You can obtain one through your local Department of Motor Vehicles. To find your local Department of Motor Vehicles, and know what documents to bring. The Real ID Act of 2012 requires you to have a birth certificate, your social security card, and two pieces of mail confirming your address and/or a lease. If you don't have any of these items, work with your case manager while you are still in prison to get a birth certificate and a social security card.

2. **Find a meeting, support group, or church to attend.** Don't do it alone! Many people who are returning to the community have a history of abusing substances like alcohol and illegal or prescription drugs. You may have participated in treatment while incarcerated, and it is important to maintain a drug-free lifestyle after release.

Ask your Drug Abuse Program Coordinator or Community Treatment Services Provider if he or she can help you find a treatment or support program before your release. If you have a supervised release plan, your Probation Officer may be able to arrange for you to participate in a substance abuse treatment program.

- Most communities have self-help support groups. Local Alcoholics Anonymous can be found at this website: www.aa.org/pages/en_US/find-local-aa. Narcotics Anonymous meetings can be found here: www.na.org/meetingsearch/.

- You can find a drug treatment facility by visiting the Substance Abuse and Mental Health Services Administration (SAMHSA) website at https://findtreatment.samhsa.gov/ or by calling the National Helpline (1-800-662-HELP/4357; 1-800-487-4889 TDD).

- The following organizations may be able to help you find other support and treatment resources in your local area:
    o National Drug Information Treatment and Referral Hotline: 1-(800)-662-HELP
    o National Mental Health Association: (703) 684-7722 voice, (800) 969-6642 info line
    o National Health Information Center: (800) 336-4797

3. **Sign-up for Health Insurance.** The Affordable Care Act has created free or low-cost health care coverage options and improved access to health care services.   If you need low-cost health insurance, go to the Health Insurance Marketplace (www. healthcare.gov). At this website individuals can find and sign up for health care coverage, and those who qualify can also sign up for Medicaid. Upon release, you have a 60-day special enrollment period to sign up. You can also call 1-800-318-2596 (TTY: 1-855-889-4325) 24/7 if you don't have a computer or need help. The phone line is closed Memorial Day, July 4th, Labor Day, Thanksgiving Day, and Christmas Day.

   o   If you need to continue medication, or medical or mental healthcare and are not able to sign up for insurance through the Health Insurance Marketplace, you need to find a community clinic that provides free or low-cost medical, mental health or dental healthcare in your area.

   o   Are you a veteran? If yes, you may qualify for healthcare through the Department of Veterans Affairs. Information about your health benefits as a veteran can be found at: http://www.va.gov/healthbenefits/apply/veterans.asp

4. **Create an email address.** Many websites (for example www.gmail.com or www.yahoo.com) allow you to set up a free email account. Make it simple and professional so that you can use it for job applications. Make a separate and distinct email address for friends or social purposes. For your professional email address, use your first name and last name, or some combination of your initials if you can. There are millions of email addresses, so the address you want may be taken. Be prepared to use another email address. For instance, if your name is Mary Martha Smith the perfect email addresses could be:

marysmith@gmail.com   marymsmith@gmail.com
mmsmith@gmail.com   msmith2018@gmail.com

Write down your email address and your password!

There is a comprehensive guide to creating an email account as well as social media tips later in this workbook.

5. **Get a debit card or bank account.** Many employers – even temp agencies - require an account to deposit your paychecks. Some larger companies will offer a payroll card that operates very much like a bank account, but it is still a good idea to open a traditional bank or credit union account and get a VISA debit card. It's nearly impossible to register for anything online without a debit card. If you can't get a checking account, an easy solution is the Walmart pre-paid debit card. You can use it like any debit or ATM card, and you can have paychecks direct deposited into it and have funds immediately available.

There are other prepaid debit cards, but they tend to have predatory pricing.

It's nice that any Walmart customer service counter can help you with your card. The Walmart card is free if you deposit more than $400/month in it or direct deposit paychecks into it. Otherwise the charge is around $4/month. You can get it in minutes at any Walmart, and it has full online access, easy to use anywhere they take debit cards, and it even has a savings account where you can stash money.

If you already have a job – ask your employer if they have a Credit Union as a company benefit. Credit Unions are great places to open your first bank account. They offer the same services as larger banks, but since they are member oriented you should get more personal service. You will have to open a "member" savings account with a low minimum deposit and then you can add additional savings and checking accounts with a debit card. They have low fees and are great places to build your credit so later – when you are ready to make major purchases like a car or a home, you will already have an established relationship to get a preapproval for a loan. You can also ask questions about this particular benefit when you are interviewing for a job.

Here's what you'll need to open a bank account or a prepaid account:

- Identification: A valid, government-issued photo ID.
- Personal information details: Name, date of birth, address, phone number, and Social Security Number.
- Money: Cash, a check, a money order, or funds you can electronically transfer into the new account.

Some banks that offer the advantage of opening a checking account online are:

- o BB&T
- o Citibank
- o Chime Bank (Online Only – no branches)
- o Chase
- o Capital One
- o Fidelity (Added benefit of having access to IRA's)

You can open an account online, and you usually have 30 days to fund it. And if you open a savings account, it will encourage you to start saving money as soon as you can. You do NOT have to order checks to open a checking account and debit cards are always free.

CHECKLIST #4 –
THINGS TO DO TO REBUILD YOUR LIFE

Do these in your first month of reentry or earlier:

1. **Take control of your finances.** To qualify for certain benefits, you will need to understand your current debts, bills, and other payments. You should already have your bank account or prepaid Walmart debit card. Work on having a simple budget. You can get budgets for free at www.daveramsey.com. Like radio host and best-selling author Dave Ramsey says, you have a budget to tell your money where to go, instead of later finding out where it went! Check out our section on Money later in this Guide.

2. **Connect with assistance programs and community organizations that can help.** Once you understand your finances, apply for benefit programs that can help you get food and other necessities. Community organizations are also ready to help.

3. **Don't forget to take care of yourself!** You have a lot going on, but make sure to stay healthy and keep on track with any medications or appointments so that you can complete all the other things you need to do.

4. **Get a free copy of your credit report.** You are entitled to a free copy of your credit report once a year. Your credit report may be used for background screening for employment and housing.

5. **Continue your education.** There are many ways to build your skills and qualify for better jobs.

6. **Begin your job search.** Getting a job is one of the hardest tasks someone with a criminal history can do. Heck, getting a job is hard enough without a criminal history. It's hard, but you can do it! There are free resources available at www.hireexfelons.org and in the book ***Illegal to Legal: Business Success for the (Formerly) Incarcerated.*** The most important thing to remember in your job search is this: **Make getting a job your job until you get a job!**

7. **Get legal assistance, if you need it.** Try to connect with organizations that do this for free. Many non-profits exist to support you if you experience discrimination or other injustice. There are many organizations that can help you request to have your civil rights reinstated (like the right to vote) or to help you have you criminal record sealed or expunged. To better understand your rights, reach out to one of these organizations or call our community support line at 877-776-2004.

    - For free tax preparation assistance irs.treasury.gov/freetaxprep

    - To estimate the value of your Earned Income Tax Credit (EITC): http://www.cbpp.org/research/ federal-tax/policy-basics-the-earned income-tax-credit

    - Managing Child Support Payments: Managing your child support requirements is incredibly important. If you have a child support order, you may be able to apply for a modification from the court to have your child support order reduced to reflect a lack of earnings or low earnings.

- You may also be eligible to participate in programs that may help you find a job, reinstate your driver's license, offer parenting education, or help reduce the amount of child support debt you owe. Legal Aid offices may be able to help with legal representation in child support cases. The contact information for Child Support offices in each state, and some tribes, can be found at: http://www.acf.hhs.gov/programs/css/resource/state-and-tribalchild-support-agency-contacts

8. **Focus on re-building healthy relationships.** Reconnecting with loved ones and having them support your transition can be incredibly empowering. However, it will take time and patience. Questions like the following, and more, are answered at www.swopbehindbars.org/money-matters on page 99.

Q: My employer says I must have direct deposit. Everywhere I go, the banks and credit unions seem to charge fees. How can I find the right account for me? Until you establish yourself, or take the time to research what's available for you in your area, you can get a Walmart prepaid card, which is free if you do direct deposit. Most credit unions will do consumer checking at no charge.

Q: My credit report has information that's wrong. How can I fix it? You can write to the credit reporting agency and dispute the charge. Check their website for instructions on how to correct erroneous r reporting.

Q: Should I borrow money from my credit card or take out a small loan to cover my bills until my next paycheck? Do the math to see which is cheapest for you. Usually a cash advance on your credit card is cheaper than a paycheck loan. Instead of getting a cash advance, can you put the bill on your credit card? Or buy a gift card with the credit card so you don't get hit with cash advance fees?

Another government website that provides tools and guidance to help manage your money is www.MyMoney.gov.

Q: What about filing taxes or getting a tax credit? If you do obtain a job, you may be eligible for a refundable tax credit (the Earned-Income Tax Credit – EITC) that encourages work and makes up for other taxes, such as payroll taxes. Millions of working families and individuals qualify for EITC; however, you must file a tax return.

CHECKLIST #5 ASSISTANCE PROGRAMS

Navigating assistance programs can be time consuming and complicated. Reach out to Community Organizations that can help you identify and apply for programs that are right for you. Try to get referrals for these organizations while you are in prison or within a few days of getting out. It makes a huge difference to have allies on release. While we have tried to include as many sources as possible, we may not have found them all. Keep your eyes open for any group, or any referral, that can help.

United Way: United Way agencies are non-profit organizations offering services to individuals and families in need. Many United Way agencies give housing assistance or referrals to supportive housing, nursing homes, and other residential programs in your area. They often know of other organizations that can help as well. In most communities, United Way agencies can be reached by dialing 2-1-1 or by going to: www.unitedway.org/find-your-united-way/.

Salvation Army: The Salvation Army has a network of shelters and programs across the nation. When available, they may be able to give lodging, clothing, food, and a cash grant for the first 90 days after you are released from RRC placement. You can find more information about the Salvation Army on their website at: www.salvationarmy.org.

Goodwill Industries International, Inc.: Goodwill helps individuals and families with education, skills training, and job placement services, as well as helps with supporting you while you look for a job. Please note that not every Goodwill has all of the services available so be sure you make a phone call before going to the location that's closet to you to make sure they offer the services that you need.

Student Loan Debt: Having a student loan in default also prevents the release of a new student loan, harming your ability to continue your education. If you're not sure about your student loans, verify your loan status.

> 1. Call the Department of Education at (800) 621-3115 or check the National Student Loan Data System website (www.nslds.ed.gov) to make sure there is no loan for you on file.
> 2. If you have a loan in default, there are several options available to you, including Income-Driven Repayment plans, to help you manage your loans.

Are you a veteran? A variety of benefits are available to individuals who have served in the United States military. For more information go to: www.benefits.va.gov/benefits/ and for housing support, call 1-877-424-3838.

Food Assistance Programs

Supplemental Nutrition Assistance Program (SNAP): The Department of Agriculture gives nutrition assistance to eligible low-income individuals and families. To receive benefits, families must meet certain financial and non-financial criteria. (Note: If you are receiving Temporary Assistance for Needy Families (TANF), you are automatically eligible.) To learn eligibility criteria and how to apply in your state, go to: http://www.fns.usda.gov/snap/apply

> Note: A federal law prohibits anyone convicted of a drug felony from receiving SNAP or TANF; however, most states have limited or eliminated that ban on services such as transportation, housing, and clothing. You can find out about Goodwill services in your area by going to: www.goodwill.org

Food Banks are excellent resources and often have access to additional services such as continuing education, health and wellness services, and counseling. You can find a food bank that is closest to you by going to http://www.feedingamerica.org/find-your-local-foodbank/ and entering your zip code.

Income Assistance Programs

There are a few income assistance programs available is the USA but they are notoriously difficult to get. It doesn't hurt to try but don't expect the process to be an easy one and you may need the assistance of an attorney that specializes in this area.

- **Temporary Assistance for Needy Families (TANF):** The Department of Health and Human Services gives employment services and cash assistance to low-income families.
- **Supplemental Security Income (SSI):** Provides money to low-income individuals who are either age 65 or older, blind, or disabled. For more information go to: www.ssa.gov/disabilityssi/ssi.html.
- **Social Security Disability Insurance (SSDI)**: Provides income to people with physical or mental problems that are severe enough to prevent them from working. Information can be found at: www.ssa.gov/disabilityssi/.

Housing Authorities. Some local housing authorities restrict access to housing for those with a criminal conviction, but many will consider any rehabilitative programming you have received, such as the Residential Drug Abuse Program (RDAP) and your family support system in their decision.

Homeless Organizations: There are organizations in almost every community that cater to homeless populations and they often have programs that will offer temporary shelter-style housing that can also help you gain access to permanent independent housing. Many shelter projects will help you find work and access childcare, education, and healthcare. They usually require a certain amount of "program participation," but if the result is that you have your own space, it might be worth investigating.

Transportation Assistance: Getting to medical appointments, job interviews, or other important meetings can be difficult if you don't have a car.

- **Public transportation** is usually the most inexpensive option, and each city and state have their own programs to help with the cost of public transportation. Your local community organization can help you navigate this. Public transit schedules are always available for free online. Special assistance such as reduced fares or services for the elderly and disabled exist as well, but you'll need to check locally for details. Many public buses and train systems have their own smart phone app, so you can plan your trips.

- **Walking/Bicycling**: If you can, plan to live within walking or bicycling distance to work, shopping, and your family.

- **Ridesharing/Carpools:** Carpools can save you money in commuting expenses. Some carpools pick up riders at their homes, meet at a place everyone agrees on, or in a commuter lot.

- **Taxi Cabs**: Typically, cabs are a convenient form of transportation; however, they can also be the most expensive. If you have a smartphone and services are available in your area, transportation apps (for example: "LyftLine," "UberX," and "UberPool") offer lower-cost options. You can learn more about these services and the costs on their websites. Downloading a transportation app to your phone and setting up an account are free.

SWOP Behind Bars

CHAPTER 3

Job Preparation

Being prepared will improve your chances of finding a job and make your job search more effective. Create an "application package" by making a draft resume using some of the tips from later in this chapter. Then collect the items you put together before you left prison (certificates, activities you completed in prison, and letters of recommendation.) Get some feedback on your resume and application package from someone who is trained in or knows how to help individuals search, prepare, and apply for jobs.

- ❑ Make a list of all the jobs you've had and companies you've worked for and approximate dates of employment in chronological order.

- ❑ Keep this list and use it to complete job applications.

- ❑ Make a list of your references. These should be people that know you and are willing to vouch for you; even if it's a case manager or counselor.

- ❑ MAKE A RESUME (functional resumes work the best for people with criminal histories – see the Resume Section).

- ❑ Make sure your background information is accurate. Many companies do screenings that may include criminal record information.

❑ HAVE A STRATEGY to deal with your criminal history on applications and in interviews (see "Great Interviews" and "Elevator Pitches" later in this Chapter).

❑ Discover the "job boards" in your area. Job boards are websites that list available jobs and includes resumes of interested applicants. You can post your resume on these boards. Avoid sites that charge, as most states' workforce development offices have free job lists you can access online.

❑ MAKE GETTING A JOB YOUR JOB UNTIL YOU GET A JOB. Don't stop looking for and applying for every job you can.

❑ It's often easier to get a job if you're employed, so don't worry if you take a job that is less than ideal. Take it, and work it until you get something better.

❑ DON'T GET DISCOURAGED by all the companies that aren't hiring you. People without criminal histories must apply for tons of jobs, and this Workbook will give you powerful tools to help make your job application process more effective.

More tips to help you prepare for your interview are located here:
http://www.careeronestop.org/JobSearch/Interview/interview-and-negotiate.aspx. Some of the basics include:

❑ Have a list of your strengths and be ready to talk about them.

❑ What are you good at?

❑ What type of work do you enjoy?

❑ When you are able, take the Clifton Strengthsfinder test from Gallup. Also check out their new employment & entrepreneurial focused assessment called the Builder Profile 10 Test. You can get codes for each test when you buy the Gallup books *Strengthsfinder 2.0* and *Born to Build*, respectively, for about $25 each. You can also buy a code for the tests at Gallup.com.

❑ What experience or skills can you offer an employer?

❑ Think about how you will answer questions about your record.

- ❑ Look at common interview questions and practice how you might answer them: www.careeronestop.org/JobSearch/Interview/common-interview-questions.aspx

- ❑ Make sure you are clean and dressed according to the job you are applying for. A local community organization or church can help you obtain clothing or other items you might need.

- ❑ Be on time. Several days before, plan how you will travel to your interview and what time you will need to leave to arrive a few minutes early.

TIPS ON MAKING A RESUME

These tips are all taken from "Killer Resume Hacks" at www.EPICCV.com. Check them out for incredible free advice on making great resumes. If you have longer employment gaps due to your incarceration, check out EpicCv's **"An Essential Step-By-Step Guide For Employment Gap Managing"** at https://epiccv.com/resume-guidelines/essential-step-by-step-guide-to-employment-gap-managing/.

The average hiring manager will look at a resume between 30 and 90 seconds, so make a memorable first impression. Use these tips to help make a resume that gets you noticed.

#1 Add accomplishments to your work experience resume section. Don't describe just what you did, but how you did it. This will give you credibility and back up your resume statements.

#2 Don't go back more than 15 years in your professional history. Nobody's interested in what you did back then. Bonus benefit: you avoid being age discriminated.

#3 Keep your past in the past. Everything about your past positions should be in past tense. Your current responsibilities should be in present tense. Finished achievements on your current job should be in past tense.

#4 Don't use an unprofessional email address in your contact details. According to a BeHiring study, unprofessional email addresses result in rejection in 76% of cases.

#5 Don't lie about your past; it's too easy for anyone to verify it in seconds. Instead have a strategy in place to manage it. You can still express yourself on the resume, and in the interview, in a way that highlights good items in your resume and diminishes bad ones.

#6 Use bullets. Don't write blocks of text. It's much easier to read information sorted in snippets of text than to grasp the whole paragraph at once.

#7 Don't use the "References available on request" sentence on your resume. Have them ready if they ask, but avoid needless fluff on your resume, which makes it easier to read and more appealing.

#8 Don't write your physical address in your resume's contact details. Nobody's going to take the absence of a physical address as a disadvantage, especially with concerns of identity theft and commuter discrimination. Besides, where you live (even if a halfway house) is no one's business.

#9 In case of an employment gap, use the Hybrid Resume Format. This format takes the best from Chronological and Functional Resume formats and combines them into an honest statement of what and when you did and emphasizes your positive sides before the gap comes into question.

#10 Always write in the third person without using pronouns in your resume. Meaning, you're not writing a novel but a resume. You don't need to use full sentences. You'll make a much better impression without using I, me, he, or she, etc.

#11 Never name your resume's filename "Resume.doc" unless you want your resume to get lost in the pile of resumes with similar file names on your recruiter's hard drive. Not only that, but your resume could easily be replaced with another one named exactly like yours. Create your file name by using use your last name, Resume Month/Year, like: "Smith Resume July 2018."

#12 *Quantify* your achievements when you can. Recruiters and hiring managers already know WHAT you did by your position title. You need to show them HOW you did it by showing relevant numbers. For example: increased sales by X%, decreased cost by $Y, etc.

#13 Use strong action verbs in the Work Experience section. Be sure to explain that you increased, improved, founded, strengthened, achieved, expanded, revitalized, built good things, decreased, reduced, resolved bad things and more.

#14 Be careful with resume length. You don't want to make a recruiter dig through your whole life story to find important stuff. You shouldn't leave out anything crucial either. Keep your resume to one or two pages maximum. Be sure to be concise.

#15 Font (type and size) in your resume matters. Stay away from Times New Roman and Arial as they are considered overused and boring. Always use fonts that can be found on every computer, are easy to read, and are not distracting. Helvetica and Garamond are good This Guide is written in the Garamond font. Don't even think about anything fancy—it distracts your reader from what you are saying.

#16 Use "Summary" instead of "Objective." Employers aren't interested in your goals. Rather, they want to know how you can help *them* reach *their* goals.

#17 In case of a short work history gap, write only years for dates of employment. By listing only years for dates of employment, you can mask a gap. This applies only if your employment gap doesn't stretch to two or more years.

#18 Don't use abbreviations in your resume, even if your industry has specific abbreviations. You never know who is looking at your resume, and not everyone knows all the abbreviations, so it's safer to avoid them all together.

#19 Include your awards, recognition, and training in the professional experience section of the resume. Doing this shows proof of your previous excellence and work ethic which may be transferred to the current job you're applying for.

#20 Make formatting simple and consistent throughout the entire resume. Headers, indents, columns, fonts, bold, use of italics, etc., should be applied consistently in all sections of your resume.

#21 Typos, grammar and punctuation mistakes WILL KILL your application, whether in resumes, on job applications, or in emails sent to apply or follow-up on the job application. Everyone makes mistakes, but these types of errors give the impression there may be an absence of commitment and lack of attention to details. Frankly it's just sloppy and irritates recruiters. Often these mistakes send your resume straight to the trash can.

#22 Don't worry about trying to make a traditional resume with all jobs listed in chronological order. Instead list the most important jobs first with the dates afterward. For instance, if you were an entry-level programmer at Google, write "Google, Programmer, dates." If you were an assistant manager at McDonald's write "McDonald's, Assistant Manager, dates."

#23 Don't be afraid to accept an entry level job you are overqualified for and then *excel* at that job. Most companies promote from within their ranks so even if you are at an entry level job at first – it doesn't mean you can't get to an executive position eventually!

The remainder of this chapter contains excerpts from the award-winning book and workbook available at Amazon: ***Illegal to Legal*** by **Bob Pelshaw**

Great Interviews & Jobs for the Formerly Incarcerated.

If you remember only one thing about how to have a great job interview, that is to **BE PREPARED**. That's what these tips are about: to prepare you for success with jobs and in life. Some of these suggestions may feel awkward to you, but the more you do them, the better you will be at them. Soon all of these will come naturally to you. These tips also work for improving your one-on-one people skills in life and in business. Using these common-sense tips will help make your job applications or interviews memorable and will get you hired more quickly!

The biggest issue most ex-offenders must deal with is how to get a job with a criminal record. Everyone has a past – not everyone is strong enough to admit it. Don't hide your past when it comes up. Since anyone can check your personal and criminal history online in seconds, why hide it or be embarrassed by it? If it's important for someone to know, then bring it up to them so they can hear your version and not see only the ugly online version.

Make a short summary statement that shares the truth about your failure but doesn't go into detail. In sales we call that an "elevator speech." It's a sales pitch designed to explain a motivating summary of your product in about the same amount of time as you are on an elevator. Deliver it in a confident, friendly, and truthful manner.

You will earn respect for bringing up your criminal history. I've had job and client interviews where the people did an online search about me and my felony before we met, and then tested me to see if I would be honest with them about it. That, and checking your social media accounts, are a normal procedure for employers before they interview you. Sincerely assure whoever you are revealing this to that your past is in the past. Be prepared to prove that statement as well. Be sorry for what you did but don't let yourself be ashamed.

The more you try to hide it, or the more shame you carry, the more you choke your ability to succeed. I don't flaunt my mistakes like a brazen hussy, but I don't hide it or have shame about it anymore because I know that I am not the same person I was. I prove that to myself and others through my daily actions: big and small, seen and unseen. We've prepared a card you can review, or leave with, potential employers titled: **"Bottom-Line Reasons to Hire the Formerly Incarcerated."**

The second biggest issue many ex-offenders must deal with is their attitude. Have a positive attitude, even if you must "fake it till you make it." Having a negative attitude, or assuming they will not hire you before you go in, just creates a self-fulfilling prophecy. You don't have to get your hopes up, but who wants to be around a negative person? Remember: your attitude will determine your altitude. And never stop trying! Every closed door means another will open so keep looking for the open door! Employers want and need you so go for it!

Here's more tips to help you nail great job interviews and great jobs:

- **LOOK AT THE COMPANY'S WEBSITE BEFORE YOUR APPLICATION OR INTERVIEW**, if you can, **to** learn about the company and the details of the position. Make notes of several things on each that you can bring up in your interview. Having knowledge of the company will increase your professionalism because it shows you are prepared and have done your homework. It will also help you decide if that job and company are something you want to commit to.

- **HAVE A LIST OF YOUR WORK HISTORY** before you go on a job interview or apply for a job. This list includes dates employed, company contact information, responsibilities, pay, and personal references. Every company will ask for the same information, so if you have it in one spot, you can complete job applications quicker and with less stress.

- **BE YOURSELF.** Be friendly, sincere, and believable, but not overbearing. Everyone can spot a phony a mile away, and employers generally avoid phonies!

- **TRY TO BRING A DECENT FOLDER WITH A NOTEPAD** that you can use to keep your resumes and work history notes, references, etc.

- **WHEN YOU MEET SOMEONE** in the company, give them a good firm handshake, try to maintain good eye contact, and always ask for a business card if they don't offer you one. Having their card makes job follow-up much easier for you, and it shows them that you are interested enough in them to ask for one.

- **HERE'S THE BEST TIP**: within the first couple minutes of hearing their name, repeat it back to them a few times until you remember it. For instance, if they ask you about your previous work history you can say "Thanks for asking Mr. Jones, my work history is…."

- **EARLY IN THE INTERVIEW** try to ask them "what exactly does the job entail, and can you please explain what a person needs to do to succeed in this job?" During the rest of the interview, try to steer your answers to the key points most interesting to the interviewer.

- **IF YOU'RE NERVOUS, JUST SLOW DOWN**, breathe deeply, and think about what you are going to say. You can even tell the person you're a little nervous and that getting this job is important to you. They will appreciate your directness and honesty, and almost always will not only make you feel more at ease, but they often will sympathize with you, or at least remember you in a good way.

- **ANSWER QUESTIONS AS DIRECTLY AS POSSIBLE,** but less is more when answering questions. Be honest, but the interviewer doesn't need you to go into too much detail. Try to think of how you would react if you were interviewing you and what you would want to know. After answering a question, you can always say in your own words "I didn't want to bore you with the details, did I answer that question completely enough for you?" Or, "Did I answer your question thoroughly? Or do you need more information from me?"

- **BE CONSIDERATE AND NEVER INTERRUPT THEM**. Show respect and appreciation.

- **TAKE NOTES WHEN THEY ARE TALKING** or answering your questions. This shows you're organized, engaged, and willing to put forth extra effort.

- **SILENCE IS OK** – there doesn't have to be constant conversation during the whole time together. Use any silence to think about the interview and how the interviewer is responding to you.

- **WATCH FOR BODY LANGUAGE** and act or react accordingly. Are they engaged and leaning forward, or are they not interested and slouching back? Are they writing down your answers? Is there head nodding in agreement?

- **PROJECT THE RIGHT BODY LANGUAGE** and be engaged, leaning forward, with eye contact. Don't slouch, be the confident professional that they need to hire instead of the bum wasting their time. If you're really good at this, you can mimic their body language signals if they are positive. That is a powerful subconscious way to get people to start accepting and considering you.

- **HAVE QUESTIONS READY** to ask them when they are done. Ask if you can ask a few questions if they haven't already offered you the chance. Before you start with your questions you can say: "I had a list of questions prepared, please give me a moment to see how many of them you've already answered." If you don't have any more questions just say, "Mr. Jones you've done a great job of answering all the questions I had."

- **MAKE SURE YOU ASK THEM** what the next step is, or when you can follow up with them about the job. Some interviewers automatically don't consider anyone that isn't interested enough in the job to find out what they have to do next.

- Here's some **"OLD SCHOOL" ADVICE** that will REALLY set you apart from the rest. Go to the Dollar store and buy a cheap packet of "thank-you" notes and mail each person who offered you an interview a short, thoughtful, handwritten note thanking them for the interview and asking them to keep you in consideration. If you can't send them a thank-you note, try to at least send them an email thanking them for the consideration.

Before I was incarcerated I never hired anyone with a criminal history. Afterwards, I sought to make a tool that applicants could use to convince employers to consider hiring them by giving employers bottom-lined reasons for them to offer jobs.

In a county where almost 30% of all citizens have some sort of a criminal history, employers hurt themselves by not considering hiring those of us with a mistake in our past. Memorize the items below so you can use them to your advantage in job applications and interviews.
- Bob Pelshaw

Bottom-Line Reasons to Hire the Formerly Incarcerated

We don't want to appeal to your humanitarian side and play the "everyone deserves a second chance" card. Instead here are ten fact-based, bottom-line enhancing, benefits of hiring formerly incarcerated citizens.

1.   Show me the money! Substantial tax credits are available for hiring citizens with a criminal history. The programs are very easy to use without a lot of red tape. Check out this site for the Federal Work Opportunity Tax Credit **www.doleta.gov/wotc**. Some states even provide partial wage reimbursement, additional tax credits, and other training funds for employers that hire felons. Check your local state's Department of Revenue and Workforce Development Office for programs where you live.

> *"We've had three (subsidies) that amounts to several hundreds of thousands of dollars to bear down on training our employees. It's amazing to me how many resources are available to a company, but they don't take the time to go after them."* Mike Hannigan, CEO of Give Something Back.

2. I need some assurances. How about some free insurance for you? Employers that hire felons can be eligible to obtain a free fidelity bond funded by the Federal government to protect you against employee dishonesty or theft. Look for the contact in your state at **www.bonds4jobs.com**. More importantly, credible studies clearly indicate that ex-offenders out of prison seven years or more have no higher rate of committing a crime than those without a criminal history. Kiminori Nakamura, assistant professor at the University of Maryland, co-authored a 2009 study that found people with a criminal record are at no greater criminal risk after they've been out seven to 10 years than those with no record. "Very old criminal records are not very useful in predicting risk," he said.

3. Does that come with a guarantee? Yep – especially if someone is on probation. Ex-offenders on probation often have to keep a job and perform well at work as a condition of their release. Most parolees are drug-tested by their probation officer or halfway house at no expense to you. Most parole officers and halfway houses welcome contact with employers of supervised citizens with a criminal history. They will refer you more workers if you let them know the type of person you want to hire. *A parole officer supervising a worker you employ = added value at no cost to you!* An estimated 6,899,000 persons were under the supervision of adult correctional systems in 2013, according to the Bureau of Justice. This is a significant, largely untapped and motivated work force.

4. What's the turnover rate? Due to the scarcity of opportunities for felons, many employers that hire those with criminal histories have lower turnover than with conventional hires. As mentioned, parole officers and halfway houses can be a great source of new workers – without the expense and trouble of placing an ad or paying a staffing agency.

5. Help reduce the cost of crime for your community. The true cost of crime exceeds millions of dollars in every county in America each year, a cost that is decreased when felons return to the work place: "People who break the law need to be held accountable and pay their debt to society. At the same time, the collateral costs of locking up 2.3 million people are piling higher and higher," said Adam Gelb, director of the Pew Center on the State's Public Safety Performance Project. According the VERA institute of Justice, the U.S. spends nearly $40 billion a year to house inmates.

6. I can't seem to find good help. That's because you haven't tried hiring felons. Considering them will enlarge the labor pool you can draw from. A 2008 study by the Urban Institute Justice Policy Center found that fewer than 45 percent of the formerly incarcerated were employed eight months after being released. That means more than three and half million workers are available. "There are costs associated but the benefits far outweigh the costs. You get a loyal employee, a motivated employee," Hannigan says.

7. Reduce crime and recidivism rates in your community. Many formerly incarcerated individuals return to crime and jail (otherwise known as recidivism) because they can't find a job. Nationally 89% of those people who were formerly arrested for returning to crime are unemployed. Please consider that employers who don't hire felons may be contributing to higher crime and recidivism.

8. Join the Crowd? Break the stigma associated with a past criminal offense. It is common to think that only "bad" people commit crimes, yet that stigma ignores the facts. NELP estimates that 70 million U.S. adults have arrest or conviction records based on Bureau of Justice statistics compiled. Tougher sentencing laws, especially for drug offenses, have swelled that total. Society can't afford to banish 70 million people from the workplace.

9. Everybody DOES NOT deserve a second chance – but some do. Those who deserve a second chance are the ones that will demonstrate, not just with words but with their actions, that they are sorry for their past mistakes and can prove that their past is in the past. Who wouldn't want to help that person?

10. What difference can I make? More than you think. Look at the costs of housing one inmate per year, compared to the economic impact of having one more productive tax-paying citizen spending money in our economy (instead of draining costs from it), and you can see hiring ex-offenders makes a HUGE difference. According to the VERA Institute of Justice, the average cost per state inmate is $31,286 per year. But if that one formerly incarcerated citizen gets a job instead of returning to prison, he or she now contributes to the economy by more than $10,000 a year, according to a Baylor University study. You can help strengthen our economy and decrease crime and recidivism by hiring a formerly incarcerated citizen.

ELEVATE YOUR FUTURE
WITH ELEVATOR PITCHES

Each Elevator Pitch should be a convincing "30 second commercial"
- Practice it until it is smooth, natural, and you are no longer nervous saying it out loud
- Keep it positive and upbeat, but realistic
- Don't complain
- Be professional

For the "Criminal History Pitch":
Be like a doctor delivering bad news: they are not emotional; they are direct, and they always tell a solution or upside. Taking responsibility, while being humble and confident, are the best ways to deliver this pitch.

Use the "Ten Bottom-Line Reasons to Hire the Formerly Incarcerated" as ammunition to help overcome their concerns about hiring someone with a criminal record.

For the "Why to Hire Me" pitch:
Listen to what they say are the job duties or what the employer says is important for the job. *Use this pitch to highlight how you fit their needs and can meet their expectations. Work to build rapport with the interviewer, creating a connection that shows you are engaged with them and this position.*

CHAPTER 4

On The Other Side Of Survival

Prison is a human zoo. A pest hole of sadness, madness and pain. This is no great news. Every person who's ever done time knows it all too well.

And a prisoner learns, too, that survival, on many levels becomes the overriding focus of his or her life. But simply "surviving" gets old — really old! So you reach a point where you ask yourself, "Why bother?" Why bother to go through this silly bullshit? Why bother to endure the same old Mickey Mouse garbage day after day, year after year? Everything gets so dirty and so dark. So why bother?

There is a reason — a very good one! In fact, there is a reward that, if understood and cultivated, can grow out of the perversion of a prison. But let's be clear: it's not simple or easy to obtain — and certainly nothing the system will be willing to share with you. And, even if it did, you wouldn't be receptive to such insight from your captor, your enemy.

It is essential to understand the deeper impact of what captivity does to the human mind and spirit. Especially how the experience forces you to narrow your vision (or "understanding") down to the madness of the moment. In so doing, it is easy to get lost in the idea that this is all there is — that this nasty, noisy, sick place is, in fact, a true reflection of what life is all about. But, you see, it simply isn't true!! Survival in a cage is NOT what life is all about. It is essential to be constantly aware there IS something on the other side of survival that stands to make it all worthwhile.

Stop and look within the very center of yourself. Come to terms with the fact that prison can never be your home, no matter how long they keep your body in a box!! There is a reason to hold on, to fight your way through, to be strong and brave, to control your mind, to refuse to surrender, to practice discipline, to cope with your rage, to maintain your dignity at any price. There is a reason – but no one wants you to know it! Why? Because the reason itself is the key to your ultimate freedom – the source of power, sanity, dignity, purpose, and pride.

This key is your sense of duty to yourself to be the very best you can be, to play the best game with the hand that has been dealt you. And to maintain your faith and efforts until you can finally reshuffle and re-deal the deck. What you must clearly understand is that imprisonment, as a long-term event, undermines and erodes your knowledge of this fact and your vision of a better day. Its real damage is not the obvious results of life in a snake pit, but how, like drinking battery acid, it eats away at your awareness of your sense of purpose – even your will to go on. So, before all else, each person must maintain his or her absolute determination to learn and grow, even on the bottom floor of hell. Guard it well – it is your greatest treasure!

Those who have been down before know full well that the rat race doesn't cease the day they kick you out of the joint. No: it simply takes on another form...and speeds up! Trying to find an answer to "why bother?" is not automatically taken care of just because they cut you loose.

So how do you effectively prepare to make it on the outside? **Begin by confronting the harsh fact that you walk out "designed to fail" on a variety of levels.**

Why? Before all else, the fantasy and illusions that incarcerated folks use to keep their heads and hearts together in prison fade away like a morning fog hit by the rays of the sun. At this point of vulnerability and panic, a person doesn't know where to go to find the motivation to carry on. It's all too easy to turn to the most ancient sources of power: rage and hostility! This is the classic action of all powerless people throughout history – a short-term remedy and a long-term curse!

Hostility, belligerence, and resentment become internal "power cells." But they are negative, dangerous, unstable and self-defeating. Yet it's often all you have, so you go with it. Unfortunately, most people are not sufficiently aware of the real influence this trap has over them. This is a big reason half of all released prisoners fail; they sabotage themselves before they have a chance to move beyond this initial stage of the battle!

Two big problems arise out of a "bad attitude": first, the world will not put up with it. In fact, you are seriously outnumbered, and, after a brief period of relative invisibility, you will be flushed, snuffed or otherwise disposed of. The other problem is the nature of rage itself; it simply burns too hot and fast to last! Like a dragster running on nitro, it's powerful in the quarter mile but useless down the road. The use of rage is the same trip; in the end it won't get you where you need to go.

Be aware: by turning to what you know best, to the spirit of hatred and revenge, to what seems most natural, to the only thing you may feel you have, you sentence yourself to hell! By this act, you surrender your body, freedom, future, and dignity to an insensitive, inhuman process that doesn't care about you, your family...or anything else.

There must be a better way, and there is!! Think of yourself standing on the bank of a wide river with your goal being to reach the other side. How will you make it across without being carried away by the current or eaten by the critters?

This is not a time for head games, self-deception, or playing dominos...its sink or swim!! Focus your mind on that which is real, true, and achievable...and be willing to pay the price, no matter how demanding, to get there. Go into training. If you don't know how to swim, you must learn. If you think that swimming wouldn't do it, build a boat. If those options don't work for you, find a ride! But whatever you do, it must pass the "reality test!!" Will it work: will it get you there!?!

All this demands a high price of faith, time, and energy. You must be strong! But, again, why bother? It always comes back to that. The answer is as simple as it is hard to hold onto: because of the beauty and joy that waits for you beyond the immediate need to "just make it through the day."

Hold on to this fact: that on the other side of survival is quality of life! Kindness, comfort, tenderness, true meaning, achievement, and an ever-growing satisfaction. Never surrender your faith in yourself or the vision of a better day – NEVER!!!

IMPACTS OF LONG-TERM CAPTIVITY

Long-term incarceration produces a mix of highly conflicting, counter-productive influences which, when combined into an overall experience, pervert participant values and diminish skills required for post-release success. These influences include:

1. An acute, ongoing grief cycle:
   - initial shock and disbelief
   - denial and minimization
   - deep-seated guilt and shame
   - all-consuming depression
   - cumulative hopelessness
   - evolving disassociation
2. An increase in psycho-social dissonance:
   - sensory deprivation
   - mental stagnation
   - loneliness and isolation
   - lethargy and desensitization
   - silent, seething desperation
   - hypertension
   - absorption: ever-shrinking universe
   - limitless longing
   - seeking artificial/micro power base
   - fear of change or any instability
   - practice of nesting behaviors
3. Distortion of reality:
   - institutionalization into prison life
   - "rewrites" nature of crime and case
   - false expectations of relief
   - contorted world view
   - a sense of entitlement
4. Post-release distress:
   - acute post-traumatic stress disorder
   - cyclical anxiety and dysfunction

Balancing Change

Change is where the rubber meets the road and where you put into practice the choices you have made. Someone once defined insanity as doing the same things expecting a different result. You may want to change, but if that desire isn't enough to make you do things differently, then don't be surprised if your life is stuck in the same rut. Change is the only way to transform your thoughts and feelings about yourself so that you can embody positive self-esteem and confidence.

This does not mean there won't be times when you are confronted with your fears of failure or success. If you are human, then you have questioned your own abilities at some point. What it does mean is that as soon as you notice you are feeling *less than* or *not enough* you will:

1. Be awake and conscious of your feelings.
2. Identify the thoughts that result in your feelings of low self-esteem or feeling down about yourself.
3. Shift your attention to thoughts supporting your ever-deepening experience of positive self-esteem. For example, what have you done recently that made you feel good about yourself? And how can you make that happen more?

Being open to change isn't necessarily about you changing who you *are*, it's about changing how you think. It's about balancing your life, accepting circumstances as they are, and being willing to adapt – especially in the beginning when all the plans you might have made don't go exactly as you planned.

On the next page is a practical tool to help you visualize a state of balance that can help you work toward bringing more calmness and stability into your life. Consider the following questions after you look at the wheel.

MY BALANCE WHEEL

1-3 Suffering
4-6 Survivng
7-10 Thriving

SPIRITUALITY & SENSE OF PURPOSE

REST & SLEEP

CREATIVITY & PLAY

GOOD NUTRITION & EXERCISE

INTELLECTUAL STIMULATION

WORK, FINANCIAL & CAREER

RELATIONSHIPS: FAMILY, FRIENDS, COMMUNITY

From Living with Intent: My Somewhat Messy Journey to Purpose, Peace and Joy, by Mallika Chopra
Pre-order the book before April 7th at www.mallikachopra.com/books and download a free meditation course.

My life could use more balance in these areas:

_____
_____
_____
_____
_____
_____
_____
_____
_____
_____

_____
_____
_____
_____
_____
_____

Some ideas for bringing balance to the areas that need it are:

_____
_____
_____
_____
_____
_____
_____
_____
_____
_____
_____
_____
_____
_____
_____
_____
_____
_____
_____
_____
_____
_____
_____
_____
_____
_____
_____

CHAPTER 5
Accepting Responsibility

This road won't be an easy one. It doesn't matter how long you've been locked up, the reentry road is not an easy one. You are going to have to work hard to never return to prison, and there are going to be challenges you didn't expect. Things you thought were solid are going to fall through. And you will be faced – more than once – with choices that don't really feel like good ones. The most difficult time is the first 90 days. The second most difficult time is every other day after that. But if you remain determined and focus on the future, each day will get easier, and in a year, you won't recognize your life from what it is today.

In two years you will start to feel more comfortable that the life you have right now is way behind you, and in five years you will know that the path you are on will lead you to a life you love living. In ten years you will probably be teaching others what you have learned, and you will be a coach that truly understands hardship and knows from experience how to turn things around.

It all starts with one thing: accepting responsibility for your life.

Accepting responsibility for your life is not about punishing yourself for the mistakes you may have made. It is accepting who you are and understanding that you are where you are because that is where you are supposed to be. We understand that we have made bad choices or find ourselves in situations we had no control over, but that doesn't mean that we are defined by our past. The past and everything that happened there is what you did, it's not who you are.

Focusing on the future and accepting that past actions may impact future decisions is the truest definition of accepting responsibility. We have no control over what has taken place in the past, and if we are constantly looking over our shoulder for the past and what it represents, we will continue to stumble, and moving forward will be difficult if not impossible.

Accepting responsibility for TODAY and making today all that it can be is how we move forward and step to our next – and better – level. Yesterday is over and cannot be changed, and tomorrow is uncertain without making positive steps today. There will be things from the past that will come up and have to be dealt with, but we must deal with them in the present with fresh eyes and better decision-making skills. We can surround ourselves with positive people and positive thoughts, and we can make an action plan for how we will live from this day forward.

Accepting responsibility for our own life also means that we no longer accept the responsibilities that others have laid at our feet that have nothing to do with our own growth. The future is yours to decide, and you must accept responsibility for how you live it. Determine what you are responsible for in your life. Set down the self-recrimination over the past and resolve to fill your own life with love, joy and peace. Forgive yourself for what you have done and forgive others for how they may have wronged you.

You have control over how you will live the rest of your life and you can choose to love every minute of every day. Don't worry about what other people may think…you have no control over their life…you only have control over yours.

Guilt and frustration and fear are the result of not letting go of baggage that you shouldn't be carrying. Set it down and welcome freedom.

Guilt and shame are two of the most common, difficult, emotions to be dealt with in healing a majority of traumatic events. These two emotions are intertwined core feelings that eat away at a person, constantly provoking Posttraumatic Stress Disorder (PTSD) symptoms. To try and separate these two emotions is useless, as one goes with the other.

What do I need to accept responsibility for?

What are Guilt and Shame?

Guilt and shame are frequently thought of as the same concept, and the terms are often used interchangeably; however, theorists have recently made a distinction between them. Both emotions involve concepts of "wrong" behavior or having done something "wrong," either by omission or commission. They also both involve negative emotions and knowledge related to the perceived offensive behavior.

Shame
Shame is a painful emotion arising from the knowing (consciousness) of something dishonorable, improper, ridiculous, disgraceful, embarrassing, etc., done by oneself or another. Shame is directly attributed to feeling

guilty about something, hence shame and guilt intertwine. Shame consists of a negative evaluation of one's own worth because he or she has acted "wrongly." Shame is conceptualized as including feelings of disgrace, disrepute, dishonor, loss of self-esteem, virtue, and personal integrity.

Guilt

Guilt is the fact of being responsible for the commission of an offense. Guilt is composed of negative emotions related to wrongdoings or perceived failures to act appropriately. Guilt includes feelings of sorrow, repentance, and disappointment in one's actions. Guilt is both a cognitive and an emotional experience that occurs when a person realizes that he or she has violated a moral standard and is responsible for that violation. A guilty conscience results from thoughts that we have not lived up to our ideal self.

According to the above definitions of both guilt and shame, it could be summarized that guilt is concentrated on one's actions, while shame is directed toward one's moral integrity and self-worth, and/or past actions and how they are perceived. In other words, a person who feels shameful may think that he or she is to blame for the immoral act and is therefore a bad person. Conversely, a person who feels guilty may believe that he or she acted wrongly and therefore feels that his or her actions were wrong, but they can still maintain a positive view of the self as a person.

Resolving Guilt

As stated above, guilt intertwines directly with the feeling of shame. Shame is a near impossible emotion to try and resolve because there is an underlying component of guilt and/or emotional cocktail. The primary resolution to shame is directly through guilt itself. The theoretical answer to understanding guilt comprises four points in order to determine the facts of a situation to change how you understand the event and your guilt associated with it. Consider the following:

1. Who owns what blame for the actual event?
2. Remove any "pre-outcome" knowledge you had convinced yourself of knowing.
3. Review the choices made under the event's actual situation, rather than hindsight.
4. Gauge moral standards /self-expectations against the facts you were aware of at the time, rather than hindsight.

Again, the theoretical answer is easy. This allows you to understand the facts based on the event itself, removing "what ifs" and "but if I only did...," which are negative thinking styles and often cloud understanding of an event itself. Focus on the event's facts rather than what you have otherwise told yourself about it.

A further problem with guilt is that many use self-blame, which invokes guilt, to reduce shame. Nasty little problem these two emotions, as they can directly become their own cycle of internal emotional abuse. You begin feeling guilty for being ashamed of something you or another did, which creates self-blame, further shame, and more guilt, and the cycle continues until you intervene within it or breakdown.

You are the only person who has the capacity to change you. External influences can only assist, guide, and provide you with knowledge or techniques. YOU must evoke the change to remove shame.

So, write about your life and decide who "owns" the blame for each event that you have unresolved guilt about. And be honest with yourself. This isn't a test and it isn't a competition. You don't have to do this all in one sitting – it will probably take you several times to unpack these emotions. And you may change your mind more than once about the ownership of the blame. Some people find it easier to write letters to themselves or to someone else, and there is nothing wrong with seeking advice from a mentor. Take it slow and make it complete. Untangle the web of events as you remember them and try to imagine yourself standing outside the event and observe the details of the situation.

While you are observing the event dispassionately – take time to remove the "what ifs and the "if onlys" – and figure out what is fact and what is what you told yourself happened. Now that you are working with FACTS and not a whirlwind of information that has built up over time, review all the choices that were made only with the information you had as the event unfolded. And finally – take stock of the situation and responsibility for your actions and set the rest of it aside. Do this exercise repeatedly and practice setting the blame aside.

What If I Own Legitimate Guilt?

Owning legitimate guilt has a positive side to it. This means that you are NOT a sociopath, and you DO have empathy, remorse and feel the correct feelings for something within your life that has gone terribly wrong.

Legitimate guilt is the most difficult type of guilt to have providing you are *at fault*, however; you cannot just assume your own guilt. You must still go through the process to ascertain what degree of blame you own, if any, and then only own that portion. Otherwise, you must assign guilt to its rightful owner.   When you own legitimate guilt, regardless of the percentage, then your options become far more limited to minimize or remove the guilt, such as:

- Forgive yourself based on the realistic and factual circumstances (age, situation, etc.).
- Accept and learn from your mistakes in order to change future choices.

Part of being a human being is that you will make mistakes. Some small, some large, and some gigantic. You DON'T need forgiveness to forgive yourself or to acknowledge your wrong doings. Making amends was NOT included in that list since, even though it can be a positive experience, entangling guilt directly with making amends can become counter-productive, or even self-abusive.

Understanding Shame
Key emotions that trigger shame are hurt, failure and helplessness. Whenever shame is present, there is guilt and other emotions. To try and tackle shame by itself is extremely difficult.

Removing Shame
Since shame is tremendously difficult to shift by itself, how do we reduce and/or remove shame? You start by dealing with the other emotions present that cause shame. Target guilt, hurt, failure, helplessness, disgust, etc., and by dealing with those emotions, shame lessens or dissipates.

What many traumatized persons confuse regarding shame, and other key emotions, is mixing past feelings with present feelings. You can heal the present, you can understand the past, but if you remember feeling shame in childhood, that is different than feeling shame now based on memories. Nothing you do now will remove your memory of feeling ashamed at an earlier period in your life. It's important to differentiate between the two. One is memory, the other is present tense. Focus on the present tense.

You may still feel ashamed of the past, you may still carry shame with you because the past has not been dealt with, though you do not have to carry shame from past events into your future for the rest of your life. Thinking about past tense may invoke the feeling of being ashamed through memories, which is different than feeling ashamed in the present.

Assertiveness and self-esteem behavioral techniques are the key to keeping shame in check in the present and future, once existing emotions have been dealt with, as most shame is associated with having low self-esteem and a passive or aggressive personality. It is extremely unlikely you'll ever find a primarily assertive person with healthy self-esteem who carries a lifetime of shame within them. It is more likely they have learned how to deal with complex emotions and communicate with people so they don't have to carry such negativity within.

Examples of Processing Shame & Guilt

Due to the complexities and significance of shame and guilt that can be associated with trauma, it would be unrealistic to not provide examples of real shame and guilt and what the process looks like to work through them. A few key situations are included below:

Family Values – Shame

As adults, we learn our values from our trusted sources, typically parents, then brothers and sisters, followed by other family/caregivers, during our upbringing. Physical abuse is not required to cause complex shame and guilt later in life, you just need screwed-up family values to achieve abuse cycles. These values can range from poverty to extremist religious beliefs, to the richest of families who avoid communication and connection.

Consider sex. Many individuals learn as children that sex is shameful. For example, they might hear: "Sex is gross, it's "bumping uglies," it's inappropriate, it's nasty, men are the only ones who like it, and anyone would be ashamed to admit a man was able to put himself inside you, that's disgusting! Being raped by an ugly man, gross! Being raped by an attractive man after you said you thought he was cute… your fault. Blame. Shame.

Some women get married so they DON'T have to have SEX anymore. I can't even relate to you, I would never come in here talking about having sex no matter how it happened. You must be more like a boy than a girl. There's something wrong with you."

Feelings/thoughts as a result: Shame. Shame. Shame. I'm not meeting their standards. I'm inadequate. I'm not natural.

Family values can become quite a toxic and complex case of negative emotional core values being instilled, which are the most difficult to change, and yet every behavior *can* be changed. Let's look at the toxicity of negative core beliefs instilling shame from childhood:

- Sex is shameful = I am at fault, guilty, if wanting or enjoying sex.

- It's gross = If I have sex, then I am disgusting.

- It's "bumping uglies" = Human organs are disgusting.

- Ashamed to admit a man was able to put himself inside you – sex is disgusting, I am disgusting for being raped, I am guilty for being raped.

- Men are the only ones who like it = I am disgusting and guilty for wanting or enjoying sex.

- Being raped by an ugly man = I am guilty of being victimized.

You can quickly see how deep the underlying negative emotions have built a core perception of disgust and guilt around sex and even men outright. What would my parents or guardians say if they found out I was gay? Perhaps even more damaging.

Negative family values can become core beliefs because you have endured them your entire life. And then in adulthood, you might discover that you are different from what the majority feel or think about these same beliefs. You discover your family inflicted their negative toxicity upon you and changing is easier said than done. Add that you are now a victim, and suddenly these existing core beliefs enhance negativity to a substantial degree, increasing feelings of shame.

Perfectionism – Shame

A very common trait within people who have suffered child abuse is perfectionism. Parents abuse a child for everything and anything, depending on their mood, so the child attempts to please them, to get it right, which is impossible to achieve. Yet this behavior becomes instinctive and the result is shame.

For example, "My shame comes from never being 'good enough'. Again, it is one thing to know it intellectually, but another to have it internalized so completely that it governs so many of my behaviors. I set impossible standards, fail to meet them, therefore I am not 'good enough', feel guilty, and the cycle repeats."

Notice how "guilty" is used in this statement. The key emotions in this statement are:

- Never being good enough = I feel like a failure.
- I set impossible standards = I fail to meet them.
- I am not good enough = I feel like a failure.
- Combined with, I feel guilty for failing to meet expectations.

When you write down your feelings or beliefs, you can then look at them and recognize key emotions, like the example above. In order to work to reduce shame, we have to target feelings of failure and guilt. When we uncover these feelings, no doubt other key emotions will also be uncovered and will lead back to the actual relationship itself. This process can be enhanced with self-esteem and assertiveness-behavior training, and with time, can resolve these feelings.

Reinforced Perfectionism – Shame For Accidents

Continuing from perfectionism, the following is an example of how retraumatization occurs within daily relationships, reinforcing negative core beliefs (perfectionism) that are already damaging and often hinder the process of positive change:

- He gave me this disgusted look – I feel failure, disgusted, embarrassment, and sadness that I let someone down I love.

- I didn't mean to, I didn't mean to – Reinforcing the feeling of failure again.

- I didn't even know – I feel guilty for not knowing something I couldn't see.

This example shows how something innocent can cause a person to feel shamed, based most likely around reinforcing prior feelings associated with abuse and the failure to be perfect.

Pleasure From Abuse
Many don't understand that the human body reacts at times, regardless of what you may want it to do. This can mean experiencing pleasure or an orgasm even though one is being raped or sexually abused at the time. Your bodily reactions are not something you can always control.

Let's pull the above statement apart to discover the underlying emotions and then we can end up with the following possible outcome:

- I must have liked it = I blame myself
- I did nothing to stop the abuse = I blame myself

Self-blame can lead to feeling guilty, which can lead to shame. And if you happen to be male, culture dictates males should be tough, strong and indestructible; and therefore, to be abused in the first place can lead to increased feelings of fault and self-blame.

Conclusion

As you can determine for yourself by now, guilt and shame go hand in hand, and are often combined with common emotions that create or enhance negative core beliefs. Shame is not an emotion you can directly target. Rather, you will always find deeper emotions beneath shame, and those are what you recognize and process. Due to its complexity, shame is not something you just remove or lose, though the aim is to reduce it so it can wither away and no longer dominate how you feel and your perception of yourself. Time will normally complete this process of removing shame completely through assertiveness and building self-esteem.

Remember that the key component to resolving both guilt and shame is to be honest with yourself and look at the deeper emotions and/or the facts of a situation, NOT what you have told yourself or have come to believe about a situation. Forums are very handy for laying out the facts of a situation, and then you can ask for honest feedback to help you determine such ownership or deeper feelings. In forums you will quickly realize you are not alone, and many other individuals have faced, and overcome, the challenges you are facing now.

A good trauma therapist or counsellor can help you. Whether you have access to a good therapist or counsellor, this workbook has some tools to help you to confront and conquer these issues. It's likely you won't solve all your issues in one setting. That's OK since that is never the goal. Starting the process is the goal. On the pages that follow, you can record your thoughts on these issues. Doing so will help you process and resolve the guilt and shame that holds you back.

What in my life causes me to feel ashamed right now? Why?

_____
_____
_____
_____
_____
_____
_____
_____
_____
_____
_____
_____
_____
_____
_____
_____
_____
_____
_____
_____
_____
_____

_____
_____
_____
_____
_____
_____
_____
_____
_____
_____
_____
_____
_____
_____

This is what I have learned from my mistakes:

_____
_____
_____
_____
_____
_____
_____
_____
_____
_____
_____
_____
_____
_____

This is how I can deal with my guilt and shame:

_____
_____
_____
_____
_____
_____
_____

_____
_____
_____
_____
_____
_____
_____
_____
_____
_____
_____
_____

It is important to have an action plan for managing future problems. Think about how you can respond in a mature, responsible, and self-affirming way when you feel ashamed of your past (or present). Now write this down! This is how I will respond when someone else tries to make me feel ashamed of my past (or present):

_____
_____
_____
_____
_____
_____
_____
_____
_____
_____
_____
_____
_____
_____
_____
_____
_____

CHAPTER 6
Journaling, Me, And "Me" Time

Journaling is by far the most effective method for chronicling the recovery process. Once things are written on paper, they become something you can deal with instead of things that keep you up at night. You probably knew this was going to be a part of the process the instant you picked up this book.

There are three important elements to journaling:

1. Journaling is a private endeavor and does not need to be shared with anyone else. Journaling is done for your own benefit and never for anyone else.

2. Journaling should be done in handwritten form to be fully effective. The physical process of documenting thoughts and feelings is what promotes problem solving and understanding of the contents. Blogging is not the same as journaling.

3. Make sure you do it regularly. Some people like to journal in the morning. Some prefer evenings and many like to take short opportunities throughout the day to note their thoughts. When you journal doesn't matter. Only that you try to do it daily.

Because journaling is private, many people worry that someone may read what they write and make judgments. To alleviate this concern, keep a separate paper supply and when you are finished writing something that you are sure you don't want to be exposed, say a simple prayer over it and tear it into the tiniest pieces you can and throw it away.

Journaling is a creative spill of your own guts and can be liberating when practiced regularly. If you find you have nothing to write, simply doodle. Many people use a life-skill workbook for inspiration. Some people find poetry to inspire their creative energy. Music can be a wonderful source of inspiration. Allow yourself to feel sorrow or fear and write down what is making you sad or afraid. The more you write, the more you will solve your inner issues. By the same token, journal about positive experiences as well. And be honest. The journaling is something to do for yourself...not for anyone else. Work it through on paper and you can work it out in life!

Can't get excited about journaling? Try an art journal and use colored pencils if you can. Art is a powerful healing tool and discovering your inner artist might help you develop a way to feel about your feelings.

Definitely journal about your intimate relationships. Get all the thoughts in your head out and on paper where they will be much more manageable.

Many times, a complicated problem or situation becomes clearer after journaling about it.

Things to Do for "Me"

Maintain Your Physical Health. Once you have health insurance, you will be able to go to any health care provider who accepts your health insurance plan. Finding a primary care physician is the best way to manage your health instead of going to the emergency room or urgent care – it will save you money and time and increase the likelihood of staying healthy. You may be referred to specialty doctors for specific health concerns. Visit these providers as soon as possible. You should also get your vision checked at least once a year, and your teeth cleaned once every six months to help prevent more serious problems in the future.

Grocery shopping can be quite a chore and can also be a big dent in your monthly budget. But, with a few tips and a little planning, you can save money at the grocery store without giving up healthy foods.

Healthy Eating on a Budget

- The key is to keep an inventory and plan your meals based on what's in season and what's on sale.

- Stock up on bulk, canned and frozen foods when they're available at a reasonable price, and buy only enough perishables to last until the next shopping trip and only if you have the space to keep it.

- Keep a Kitchen Inventory and plan meals before you shop.

- Look in your kitchen cabinets to see what you've got on hand. Make a list of everything you find, either on a sheet of paper or digitally (notes apps on smartphones work perfectly for this so you don't have to worry about leaving your list at home).

- Make a full meal plan for the week, or at least think about some of the foods you plan on preparing, or what you like to have on hand.

- Look at the ads for your local grocery store or look at their website to see what's on sale. Mix and match your meals so you can make the most of the least expensive items.

When you plan your meals, choose several recipes that use the same perishable ingredients. For example, if chicken breasts are on sale, plan on roasted chicken breasts one night and chicken Caesar wraps later in the week. Or prepare a spinach salad one night and sautéed spinach the next.

Don't Forget to Plan for Leftovers

Stretch your dollars by planning meals for your leftovers. For example, maybe roast beef is on sale, and you don't want three nights of it. Go ahead and prepare some homemade frozen meals that you can store in the freezer. Freeze your foods in microwave-safe containers or make foil pouches that can be popped into the oven.

It takes some time, but planning your meals can save you money and make your shopping trip easier. Here are plenty of tips to get you started:

- Buy a water filter pitcher instead of expensive individual bottles of water.
- Buy bulk items when they are on sale. Same with canned goods, frozen vegetables, fish, and seafood.
- Buy a whole chicken and cut it up yourself.

- When meats are on sale, you can buy larger quantities and freeze individual pieces in the freezer.
- Use freezer paper or freezer bags so you don't end up with freezer burn.
- Look for coupons online and in newspapers and magazines.
- Use dry beans as a protein source because they are much cheaper than meats (think black beans in your burritos instead of beef).
- Fresh produce is often a good buy, especially when in season, but choose carefully and don't buy more than what you'll be able to consume within a few days. You don't want to waste any due to spoilage.
- Look for different ways to prepare your foods so your meals don't get dull. Potatoes can be baked or boiled one night and maybe roasted or mashed the next night.
- Keep your salads interesting by changing up vegetables and toppings.
- Skip the convenience foods because they're expensive and often not all that healthy.
- Choose cheaper, leaner cuts of beef. You'll reduce saturated fat and save money.
- The cheaper cuts of beef need to be cooked at lower temperatures and over longer periods of time, so they're good for soups and stews.
- Make your own snacks with mixed nuts, dry cereals, raisins and other ingredients.
- Divide the snacks into individual portions and keep them in bags to control calorie intake.
- Explore Once a Month Cooking. With this method, you prepare a month's worth of meals in one weekend. Perfect if you have a larger freezer.

Exercise on a Budget

Exercise is good for your body and your mind! You can stave off depression with a brisk walk, and the gym is a great place to make new friends. It's difficult to get in the habit of exercising regularly, but you will be glad you stayed active if you give it some time.

When you're on a budget, you must get creative with your spending habits, and signing up for a pricey gym or class membership is not on your list of splurges. For those who still want to exercise, however, there are inexpensive ways to try that new cycling class you've been obsessing over or that CrossFit workout everyone's talking about. And yes, you can definitely work toward that Beyoncé body without spending an insane amount of money on a personal trainer. Read on to see all the creative ways you can stay fit while maintaining the budget you have set for yourself.

1. **Search for studios that offer a free first class.** Often small studios will let guests take the first class for free. Interested in cycling classes? Do a quick search in your neighborhood and you'll come across places like Peloton, where riders ride for free their first time. If you're a yogi, check out Yoga to the People. With various locations in cities like San Francisco and New York, this spot is great for those who want to pop in for a quick class. The suggested donation method lets yoga-lovers pay anywhere from $1 to $10, which is a steal (and practically free).

2. **Start a running or hiking club.** As the weather gets warmer, opt for a run or hike with a friend. You can go at your own pace, and sweating it out with a BFF is always more fun than working out alone.

3. **Go swimming at the beach or outdoor pool.** Summer is the perfect time to do outdoor activities like swimming. Take a dip in a friend's pool or head to the nearest beach for a swim. You won't even feel like you're exercising.

4. **Sign up for free gym passes.** Crunch, David Barton, Equinox, and Gold's Gym all offer three- to seven-day free passes to guests. If you don't want to commit to one gym spot, these free passes are your jackpot. You can also strategically plan which gyms to visit using the free passes, which adds up to almost a free month of exercising. And Planet Fitness is a nationwide chain that charges as little as $10 a month for a budget membership.

5. **Search for fitness videos on YouTube.** YouTube channels Blogilates, BeFit, and POPSUGAR Fitness let you work out in the comfort of your own home. Without spending any money, you can exercise alongside top-notch trainers Jillian Michaels, Kym Johnson, and Denise

Austin on BeFit. If you crave a more scenic workout, Tone It Up will make you feel like you're at the beach. Invite friends over for a group workout, and then reward yourselves with sweet post-workout snacks that replenish energy and rebuild muscles.

6. Check out fitness websites with free trials.
. Pilatesology and YogaGlo offer free 10- to 15-day free trials. You can stream the classes online, which is perfect for those who are always on the go or hate the gym. The virtual classes allow you to work out anywhere, anytime.

7. Attend local free fitness events. Facebook is surprisingly a great place to find free fitness events — outdoor yoga, anyone? — in your area. Go to your events tab and scroll down to Events Popular in Your Network and Popular Events Nearby. You can even check out which events your friends will be attending.

8. Search Groupon and LivingSocial for gym deals. No need to splurge on an expensive gym membership. Groupon and LivingSocial offer the most comprehensive discounts for all your fitness needs, from CrossFit to Zumba to personal trainers.

9. Play sports at public courts. Take advantage of free outdoor basketball or tennis courts. Organize a game among a group of friends, or head to the courts yourself to meet new people.

10. Walk dogs for adoption shelters. It's not even exercise if you get to play with a fluffy puppy, right? Most shelters need volunteers to walk their dogs, and places like the ASPCA only require eight hours per month as a time commitment.

Getting Enough Sleep
Here are nine powerful benefits to getting enough sleep
   1. Better health. Getting a good night's sleep won't grant you immunity from disease, but study after study has found a link between insufficient sleep and some serious health problems, such as heart attacks, diabetes, and obesity.

   In most cases, the health risks from sleep loss only become serious after years. That might not always be true, however. One study simulated the effects of the disturbed sleep patterns of shift workers on 10 young healthy adults. After a mere four days, three of them had blood levels that qualified as pre-diabetic.

2. Better sex life. According to a poll conducted by the National Sleep Foundation, up to 26% of people say that their sex lives tend to suffer because they're just too tired. There's evidence that in men, impaired sleep can be associated with lower testosterone levels, although the exact nature of the link isn't clear. Of course, not getting enough sleep can affect your love life in less direct ways too. If you're a 28-year-old who's so exhausted you're falling asleep during a date at the movies, that's not good.

3. Less pain. If you have chronic pain – or acute pain from a recent injury – getting enough sleep may actually make you hurt less. Many studies have shown a link between sleep loss and a lower pain threshold. Unfortunately, being in pain can make it hard to sleep. Researchers have found that getting good sleep can supplement medication for pain. If pain is keeping you up at night, there are also medications available that combine a pain reliever with a sleep aid.

4. Lower risk of injury. Sleeping enough might keep you safer. Sleep deprivation has been linked with many notorious disasters, like the destruction of the space shuttle Challenger and the grounding of the Exxon Valdez. The Institute of Medicine estimates that one out of five auto accidents in the U.S. results from drowsy driving – that's about 1 million crashes a year. Of course, any kind of accident is more likely when you're exhausted. When you're overtired, you're more likely to trip, or fall off a ladder, or cut yourself while chopping vegetables. Household accidents like that can have serious consequences.

5. Better mood. Getting enough sleep won't guarantee a sunny disposition, but you have probably noticed that when you're exhausted, you're more likely to be cranky. That's not all. Not getting enough sleep affects your emotional regulation. When you're overtired, you're more likely to snap at your boss, or burst into tears, or start laughing uncontrollably.

6. Better weight control. Getting enough sleep could help you maintain your weight – and conversely, sleep loss goes along with an increased risk of weight gain. Why? Part of the problem is behavioral. If you're overtired, you might be less likely to have the energy to go for that jog or cook a healthy dinner after work. The other part is physiological. The hormone leptin plays a key role in making you feel full. When you don't get enough sleep, leptin levels drop. Result: people who are tired are just plain hungrier — and they seem to crave high-fat and high-calorie foods specifically.

7. Clearer thinking. Have you ever woken up after a bad night's sleep feeling fuzzy and easily confused, like your brain can't get out of first gear. Sleep loss affects how you think. It impairs your cognition, your attention, and your decision-making. Studies have found that people who are sleep-deprived are substantially worse at solving logic or math problems than when they're well-rested. They're also more likely to make odd mistakes, like leaving their keys in the fridge by accident.

8. Better memory. Feeling forgetful? Sleep loss could be to blame. Studies have shown that while we sleep, our brains process and consolidate our memories from the day. If you don't get enough sleep, it seems like those memories might not get stored correctly — and can be lost. What's more, some research suggests that sleep decreases the chances of developing false memories. In several experiments, people were asked to look over a series of words. Later they were tested on what they remembered. People who didn't sleep in between were much more likely to "remember" a word that they hadn't seen before.

9. Stronger immunity. Could getting enough sleep prevent the common cold? One preliminary study put the idea to the test. Researchers tracked over 150 people and monitored their sleep habits for two weeks. Then they exposed them to a cold virus. People who got seven hours of sleep a night or less were almost three times as likely to get sick as the people who got at least eight hours of sleep a night. More research is needed to establish a real link; this study was small and other factors may have influenced the results. Still, you can't go wrong getting eight hours of sleep when possible.

"Me Time."

"Me time" is necessary to succeed at journaling. You might be thinking the same thing I thought when someone introduced the concept of "me time" to me. I thought *"Seriously? The only way I'm going to ever get any me time is if there are more hours in the day!"* Nobody wants extra hours in prison. The days go slow enough!

But it's important — especially as your release date closes in — to really get yourself centered and focused on your future, you've got a lot to do and the release date will come quicker than you think! You must start making plans and coordinating what needs to be done the first few weeks you are free. It's not easy to make "me time" a priority!

A lot of us are nurturers. And yet in our desire to "take care" of those around us, we often fail to take care of ourselves. It is so much easier to address the problems of others rather than focus on what needs to be worked on within us. Scheduling time for ourselves is not a selfish act. We cannot help others if we are failing ourselves.

"Me Time" can be as little as 15 minutes when you begin. You can work toward a goal of spending two hours a day focusing on the issues that are within you. You can spend this time journaling, reading, or simply enjoying time alone with your thoughts. You can listen to inspirational music or the sounds of nature. You can daydream about the future. You can cry about the past.

"Me Time" is exactly what it implies. Time to reflect on your life as it was, as it is and what you want it to be.

There are many mental exercises you can use to get used to the idea of spending time alone with your thoughts. A favorite of many is to mentally create the life they would like to have. Imagine the kind of job you would love to go to work at every day. Think about what you would wear and where you would live. Think about the kind of car you would drive and how you would spend your free time.

When you start to "see" the images in your mind, complete the process by writing it down or drawing pictures that reflect your wishes, hopes and dreams. If our mind can "see" it, it starts to "believe" it, and we are free to achieve it. Don't worry if your vision changes as you progress. Embrace the new circumstances and continue to dream about what is to come.

Fill yourself up FIRST and it will be completely natural for you to be able to reach out and give away what is overflowing from you. We can't give away what we don't have!

How can I make "me time"?

_____
_____
_____
_____
_____
_____
_____

_____
_____
_____
_____
_____
_____
_____
_____
_____
_____
_____
_____
_____
_____
_____
_____
_____
_____
_____
_____
_____
_____
_____
_____

What can I do to start journaling, and when can I do it?

_____
_____
_____
_____
_____
_____
_____
_____
_____
_____
_____
_____
_____
_____
_____
_____
_____

_____
_____
_____
_____
_____
_____
_____
_____
_____
_____
_____
_____
_____
_____
_____
_____
_____
_____
_____
_____
_____
_____

Why wait to start journaling? Here are some sheets you can start with:

_____
_____
_____
_____
_____
_____
_____
_____
_____
_____
_____
_____
_____
_____
_____
_____
_____

CHAPTER 7
Getting Goals to Work for You

Many people feel as if they're adrift in the world. They work hard, but they don't seem to get anywhere worthwhile. They seem to be living proof of something else Coach Wooden said: *Activity does not always equal accomplishment.*

A key reason that they feel adrift or unfocused is that they haven't spent enough time thinking about what they want from life and haven't set formal goals for themselves. After all, would you set out on a major journey with no real idea of your destination? Probably not!

Goal setting is a powerful process for thinking about your ideal future and for motivating yourself to turn your vision of this future into reality. The process of setting goals helps you choose where you want to go in life. By knowing precisely what you want to achieve, you know where you must concentrate your efforts. You'll also quickly spot the distractions that can, so easily, lead you astray.

Why Set Goals?
Goal setting is used by top-level athletes, successful business-people and achievers in all fields. Setting goals gives you long-term vision and short-term motivation. It focuses your acquisition of knowledge and helps you to organize your time and resources so that you can make the very most of your life.

By setting sharp, clearly-defined goals, you can measure and take pride in the achievement of those goals, and you'll see forward progress in what might previously have seemed a long pointless grind. You will also raise your self-confidence as you recognize your own ability and competence in achieving the goals that you've set.

Clearly defined goals are not necessarily written in stone, but opportunity knocks at the door of people who are actively working toward something. Your goals will shift and develop over time and you grow and develop. The key is recognizing that you need a path...and a plan for walking the path.

Starting to Set Personal Goals

You set your goals on many levels. First, you create your "big picture" of what you want to do with your life (or over, say, the next 10 years), and identify the large-scale goals that you want to achieve. Then, you break these down into the smaller and smaller targets that you must hit to reach your lifetime goals. Finally, once you have your plan, you start working on it to achieve these goals.

Therefore, we start the process of goal setting by looking at your lifetime goals. Then, we work down to the things that you can do in, say, the next five years, then next year, next month, next week, and today, to start moving towards them.

Step 1: Setting Lifetime Goals

The first step in setting personal goals is to consider what you want to achieve in your lifetime (or at least, by a significant and distant age in the future). Setting lifetime goals gives you the overall perspective that shapes all other aspects of your decision making. To give a broad, balanced coverage of all important areas in your life, try to set goals in some of the following categories (or in other categories of your own, where these are important to you):

Career - What level do you want to reach in your career or business, or what do you want to achieve?

Financial - How much do you want to earn, by what stage? How is this related to your career goals?

Education - Is there any knowledge you want to acquire in particular? What information and skills will you need to have to achieve other goals?

Family - Do you want to be a parent? Or are you already a parent? If so, do you have custody of your child/children? How are you going to be a good parent? How do you want to be seen by a partner or by members of your extended family?

Artistic - Do you want to achieve any artistic goals?

Attitude - Is any part of your mindset holding you back? Is there any part of the way that you behave that upsets you? If so, set a goal to improve your behavior or find a solution to the problem. Your attitude will determine your altitude.

Physical - Are there any athletic goals that you want to achieve, or do you want good health deep into old age? What steps are you going to take to achieve this?

Pleasure - How do you want to enjoy yourself? (You should ensure that some of your life is for you!)

Public Service - Do you want to make the world a better place? If so, how?

Spend some time brainstorming these things, and then select one or more goals in each category that best reflect what you want to do. Then consider trimming again so that you have a small number of significant goals that you can focus on.

As you do this, make sure that the goals that you have set are ones that you genuinely want to achieve, not ones that your parents, family, or employers might want. (If you have a partner, you probably want to consider what he or she wants - however, make sure that you also remain true to yourself!)

Step 2: Setting Smaller Goals

Once you have set your lifetime goals, set a five-year plan of smaller goals that you need to complete if you are to reach your lifetime plan. Then create a one-year plan, six-month plan, and a one-month plan of progressively smaller goals that you should reach to achieve your lifetime goals. Each of these should be based on the previous plan.

Then create a daily list of your top priorities you must do today. Don't try to put everything on your list, or it will become unmanageable and overwhelming, and it won't be a useful tool for you. Instead put on your To-Do List things that you can do today to work towards your lifetime goals. At an early stage, your smaller goals might be to read books and gather information on the achievement of your higher-level goals. This will help you to improve the quality and realism of your goal setting. Review your plans, and make sure that they fit the way in which you want to live your life.

The Key to Succeed: Manage Your Goals.

If you've made, and broke, a new year's resolution, then you know that making goals isn't enough. The key is *managing* the goals you've already made. A goal without proper management is just a dream without enough desire to make it real. Once you've decided on your first set of goals, keep the process going by reviewing and updating your To-Do List daily. Periodically review the longer-term plans and modify them to reflect your changing priorities and experience. (A good way of doing this is to schedule regular, repeating reviews using a computer-based diary.)

Another Key: Use SMART Goals.

A useful way of making goals more powerful is to use the SMART mnemonic. While there are plenty of variants (some of which we've included in parenthesis), SMART usually stands for:

    S - Specific (or Significant).

    M - Measurable (or Meaningful).

    A - Attainable (or Action-Oriented).

    R - Relevant (or Rewarding).

    T - Time-bound (or Trackable).

For example, instead of having "sailing around the world" as a goal, it's more powerful to say, "to have completed my trip around the world by December 31, 2025." Obviously, this will only be attainable if a lot of preparation has been completed beforehand!

Further Goal Setting Tips.

The following broad guidelines will help you to set effective, achievable goals:

- **State each goal as a positive statement**. Express your goals positively – "Execute this technique well" is a much better goal than "Don't make this stupid mistake."
- **Be precise**. Set precise goals, putting in dates, times and amounts so that you can measure achievement. Doing this lets you know when you have achieved the goal, so you can celebrate it!

- **Set priorities**. When you have several goals, give each a priority. This helps you to avoid feeling overwhelmed by having too many goals and helps you focus on the most important ones. Having priorities make it easier to say no to things that distract you from your goals.

- **Write your goals down.** This crystallizes them and gives them more force. It also gives you accountability that your goals have value and should be met.

- **Keep operational goals small**. Keep the low-level goals that you're working towards small and achievable. If a goal is too large, then it can seem that you are not making progress towards it. Keeping goals small and incremental gives more opportunities for reward.

- **Set performance goals, not outcome goals.** Set goals with things you can control. It's disappointing to miss goals for reasons beyond your control. In business, these reasons could be bad business environments or unexpected effects of government policy. In sport, they could include poor judging, bad weather, injury, or just plain bad luck. If you base your goals on personal performance, then you can keep control over the achievement of your goals and draw satisfaction from achieving them.

- **Set realistic goals**. It's important to set goals that you can achieve. All sorts of people (for example, employers, parents, media, or society) can set unrealistic goals for you. They will often do this in ignorance of your own desires and ambitions. It's also possible to set goals that are too difficult because you might not appreciate either the obstacles in the way or understand quite how much skill you need to develop to achieve a level of performance.

Using Well-Formed Outcomes in Goal Setting.

When you've achieved a goal, take the time to enjoy the satisfaction of having done so. Absorb the implications of the goal achievement and observe the progress that you've made towards other goals. If the goal was a significant one, reward yourself appropriately. All of this helps you build the self-confidence you deserve. With the experience of having achieved this goal, review the rest of your goal plans.

If you achieved the goal too easily, make your next goal harder. If the goal took a dispiriting length of time to achieve, make the next goal a little easier. If you learned something that would lead you to change other goals, do so. If you noticed a deficit in your skills despite achieving the goal, decide whether to set goals to fix this. Failing to meet goals does not matter if you learn from the experience.

Your goals will change as time goes on. Adjust them regularly to reflect growth in your knowledge and experience, and if goals do not hold any attraction any longer, consider letting them go. Whatever method you use for tracking your thoughts and planning your life, stick to the plan and don't get distracted by the outside influences that get you hung up and unable to move forward. Setting the goals is a great and important step in the process of Living a Life You Love, but the goal is always to achieve the goals you set for your life.

What are your lifetime goals in the following areas?

Career - What level do you want to reach in your career or business, or what do you want to achieve?

_____
_____
_____
_____
_____
_____
_____
_____
_____
_____
_____
_____
_____

Financial - How much do you realistically want to earn, and by what stage in your life? How is this related to your career goals?

_____
_____
_____
_____
_____
_____
_____
_____

_____
_____
_____
_____
_____
_____
_____
_____

Education - Is there any knowledge you want to acquire in particular? What information and skills will you need to have to achieve other goals?

_____
_____
_____
_____
_____
_____
_____
_____
_____
_____
_____
_____
_____

Family - Do you want to be a parent? Are you already a parent? If so, how are you going to be a good parent? How do you want to be seen by a partner or by members of your extended family?

_____
_____
_____
_____
_____
_____
_____
_____
_____
_____
_____
_____
_____

Artistic - Do you want to achieve any artistic goals?

_____
_____
_____
_____
_____
_____
_____
_____
_____
_____
_____
_____
_____
_____
_____
_____

Attitude - Is any part of your mindset holding you back? Is there any part of the way that you behave that upsets you? If so, set a goal to improve your behavior or find a solution to the problem. Your attitude will determine your altitude.

_____
_____
_____
_____
_____
_____
_____
_____
_____
_____
_____
_____
_____
_____

Physical - Are there any athletic goals that you want to achieve, or do you want good health deep into old age? What steps are you going to take to achieve this?

_____
_____
_____

_____
_____
_____
_____
_____
_____
_____
_____
_____
_____
_____
_____

Pleasure - How do you want to enjoy yourself? (You should ensure that some of your life is for you!)

_____
_____
_____
_____
_____
_____
_____
_____
_____
_____
_____
_____

Public Service - Do you want to make the world a better place? If so, how?

_____
_____
_____
_____
_____
_____
_____
_____
_____
_____
_____
_____

Knowing these are my lifetime goals, my five-year goals are:

My one-year goals are: _____
_____
_____
_____
_____
_____
_____

My six-month goals are: _____
_____
_____
_____
_____
_____

Do you have a hard time thinking 10 years in the future? You are NOT alone! While it's REALLY important to have long term and short term goals, sometimes it's hard to dream past the survival stage so try breaking the long term goals down into 90 Day segments and be super SPECIFIC. In other word – don't just say you want to get a job in 90 days – break it down into manageable (and ACHIEVALBE) segments such as writing a resume, creating a profile on Job Search engines, uploading the resume to the job search engines, email prospective employers or determine what jobs – or potential businesses – are within a 5 mile radius of your location. Then set another 90 day goal – like apply for 3 jobs a day, or get 1 interview a week – work to meet the goals on the shorter list.

My 90 Day Goals are:
1.

2.

3.

4.

5.

6.

7.

8.

9.

10.

My one-month goals are:

_____
_____
_____
_____
_____
_____
_____
_____
_____
_____
_____
_____
_____
_____
_____
_____
_____
_____
_____
_____
_____

Break down the one-month goals into separate one-week goals.
Week 1 goals:

_____
_____
_____
_____
_____
_____
_____

_____
_____
_____

Week 2 goals:

_____
_____
_____
_____
_____
_____
_____
_____
_____
_____

Week 3 goals:

_____
_____
_____
_____
_____
_____
_____
_____
_____
_____

Week 4 goals:

_____
_____
_____
_____
_____
_____
_____
_____
_____
_____

CHAPTER 8
Mind Mapping & The List

Mind Mapping is an important technique that improves the way you record information and supports and enhances your creative problem solving. By using Mind Maps, you can quickly identify and understand the structure of a subject. You can see the way that pieces of information fit together, as well as recording the raw facts contained in normal notes. More than this, Mind Maps encourage creative problem solving, as they hold information in a format that your mind finds easy to remember and quick to review.

Mind Maps abandon the list format of conventional note taking. They do this in favor of a two-dimensional structure. A good Mind Map shows the 'shape' of the subject, the relative importance of individual points, and the way in which facts relate to one another. Mind Maps are more compact than conventional notes, often taking up one side of paper. This format helps you to make associations easily. If you find out more information after you have drawn the main Mind Map, then you can easily integrate it with little disruption.

Mind Maps are also useful for:
- Summarizing information.
- Consolidating information from different research sources.
- Thinking through complex problems.

They are very quick to review because you can often refresh information in your mind just by glancing at one. And in the same way, they can be effective mnemonics: Remembering the shape and structure of a Mind Map can give you the cues you need to remember the information within it. As such, they engage much more of your brain in the process of assimilating and connecting facts compared with conventional notes.

To make notes on a subject using a Mind Map, draw it in the following way:

1. Write the title of the subject you're exploring in the center of the page, and draw a circle around it.
2. As you come across major subdivisions or subheadings of the topic (or important facts that relate to the subject) draw lines out from this circle. Label these lines with these subdivisions or subheadings.
3. As you "burrow" into the subject and uncover another level of information (further subheadings, or individual facts) belonging to the subheadings above, draw these as lines linked to the subheading lines.
4. Finally, for individual facts or ideas, draw lines out from the appropriate heading line and label them.
5. As you come across new information, link it in to the Mind Map appropriately.

A complete Mind Map may have main topic lines radiating in all directions from the center. Sub-topics and facts will branch off these main topic lines, like branches and twigs from the trunk of a tree. You do not need to worry about the structure produced, as this will evolve of its own accord.

Your Mind Maps are your own property: once you understand how to make notes in the Mind Map format, you can develop your own conventions to take them further. The following suggestions may help to increase their effectiveness:

*   **Use single words or simple phrases for information**: Most words in normal writing are padding, and they ensure that facts are conveyed in the correct context and in a format that is pleasant to read. In your own Mind Maps, single strong words and meaningful phrases can convey the same meaning more potently. Excess words just clutter the Mind Map.

- **Print words**: Joined up or indistinct writing can be more difficult to read.

- **Use color to separate different ideas**: This will help you to separate ideas where necessary. It also helps you to visualize the Mind Map for recall. Color also helps to show the organization of the subject.

- **Use symbols and images**: Where a symbol or picture means something to you, use it. Pictures can help you to remember information more effectively than words.

- **Using cross-linkages**: Information in one part of the Mind Map may relate to another part. Here you can draw in lines to show the cross-linkages. This helps you to see how one part of the subject affects another.

If you like using a computer, there are many mind mapping programs that are free and low cost and give you a lot of flexibility for really fleshing out goals and objectives.

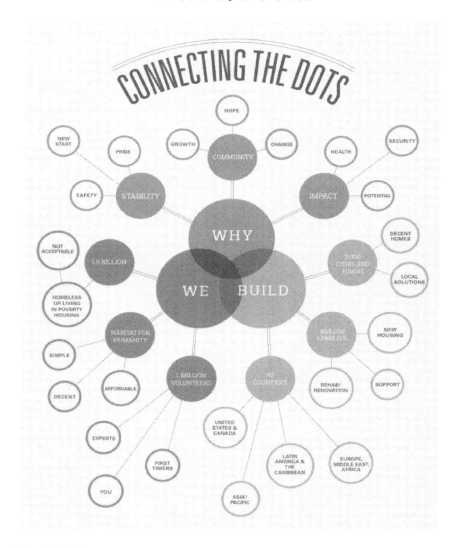

The "List"

Procrastination is one of the quickest ways we can defeat ourselves. Especially when we procrastinate doing the things that are necessary to keep our lives running smoothly. Playing catch up and fighting that bug we all have to over-commit is a daily struggle. Practice makes perfect, and if we put simple tools in place to keep track of our goals, responsibilities and track our progress, we become proficient at managing our lives.

Whether it be a phone call or an action, getting our lives in order – and keeping them in order - means that we must get our "stuff" taken care of. A great tool to use is as easy as getting a notebook and a pen.

Draw a line down the middle of the page and label one side "PHONE CALLS" and the other side "ACTIONS". Start to list all the phone calls you need to make to either complete a task or to get more information or even to make an appointment. The phone calls list will bring about an action and you will list the action and cross off the phone call that you completed.

When you complete an action, you can cross that off the list, being sure that if you need a follow up action, you put it at the end of the ACTION list. It helps to have a calendar available so you can post specific appointments or target dates for the completion of a goal, but don't let the calendar run your life. The list is more than adequate to keep your life in line. "The List" is a working document that shows you what you need to do while letting you know what you've done. Don't be afraid to pat yourself on the back as you cross things off.

The list is important for two reasons. One – it helps you to see what you need to do on paper instead of just creating worry and frustration. Second, crossing things off your list creates a feeling of accomplishment and well-being. You can be proud of what you have accomplished as well as mindful of what you need to stay on top of.

Use the list in conjunction with your written goals and as time goes on, your decision-making skills will improve and become second nature. Trust your instincts and stay true to the things you believe in.

The List

PROS	/	CONS

CHAPTER 9
Decisions and Boundaries

Goals don't get met without a decision to take the steps to meet them. Lives don't change until there is a decision to change.

Making better decisions virtually guarantee that a life can be led without drama and chaos constantly interfering with the peace that we have worked so hard to construct. There are many formulas for making decisions. Some are drawn out and complicated and require flow charts as to who gets what information and when they get it.

There are a lot of factors that go into making decisions for real life situations. Many people find it helpful to make a list of Pros and Cons, but just because one side or the other is longer does not necessarily mean that is the right way to go. Each Pro or Con must carry a "weight" based on its overall importance to the desired goal. You must follow the basics of decision making by setting a goal, assembling all the information and asking your three critical questions.

1. Will this decision improve my life in the short term?
2. Will this decision improve my life over the long term?
3. How will this decision impact the next year of my life?

It never hurts to ask for advice from someone who is outside of the situation and is not benefitting from the results of your situation. It is a wise person who can take counsel.

At the end of the day, when you have made a decision, you must act on your decision, take responsibility for the results, and be willing to change your mind as circumstances dictate. Don't be afraid to "play the tape all the way through" and really explore the impact of decisions on your own life and the lives of your friends and family.

Setting and Respecting Boundaries

I first learned of the concept of personal boundaries from the excellent book ***Boundaries: When to Say Yes and When to Say No to Take Control of Your Life*** by Dr. Henry Cloud and Dr. John Townsend. Read it if you can. The book starts with the analogy of the property line at your home. Even if you've never surveyed it, everyone knows where their property line is. You wouldn't let your neighbor store their trash in your yard, would you? You wouldn't try to store your trash in their yard either. Those are boundaries most people wouldn't cross.

In the book ***Boundaries,*** the authors assert that most any relationship issue we have with anyone else, and many of our problems, are due to our failure to establish, respect, or defend a boundary in our lives and relationships. Establishing (communicating), respecting, and defending boundaries are a daily decision you must continually and regularly do.

Personal boundaries are a necessary tool in negotiating your way through life. They are determined by your own moral and ethical code of conduct. It is important to not only learn to set your own personal boundaries about what behaviors, attitudes and preferences you will - and will not - accept, but to also balance that with the ability to respect the boundaries of others.

We live in a world of many different people and many different cultures, some of which we may not agree with. This doesn't mean that we impose our own feeling on others. It means that many times we will agree to disagree. This respecting of other people's boundaries is a personal choice and is based on the biblical principle of "Judge not lest you be judged."

First, commit to doing no harm. This is the same oath that doctors must swear to before being granted a license to practice medicine.

Second, be a person of your word. If you say you are going to do something, then make every effort to make sure that you follow through with the commitment you made.

Third, command – not demand – respect by the way you live your own life. Treat others as you would like to be treated. This does not guarantee that you will be treated well, but it will certainly allow you to determine if someone who is treating you badly needs to be a part of your life.

Healthy Personal Boundaries & How to Establish Them

Learning to set healthy personal boundaries is necessary for maintaining a positive self-concept, or self-image. It is our way of communicating to others that we have self-respect, self-worth, and will not allow others to define us.

Personal boundaries are the physical, emotional and mental limits we establish to protect ourselves from being manipulated, used, or violated by others. They allow us to separate who we are and what we think and feel from the thoughts and feelings of others. Their presence helps us express ourselves as the unique individuals we are, while we acknowledge the same in others.

It would not be possible to enjoy healthy relationships without the existence of personal boundaries, or without our willingness to communicate them directly and honestly with others. We must recognize that each of us is a unique individual with distinct emotions, needs and preferences. This is equally true for our spouses, children and friends.

To set personal boundaries means to preserve your integrity, take responsibility for who you are, and to take control of your life.

How do we establish healthy personal boundaries?

You have a right to personal boundaries. You not only have the right, but you must take responsibility for how you allow others to treat you. Your boundaries act as filters permitting what is acceptable in your life and what is not. If you don't have boundaries that protect and define you, as in a strong sense of identity, you tend to derive your sense of worth from others. To avoid this situation, set clear and decisive limits so that others will respect them and then be willing to do whatever it takes to enforce them. Interestingly, it's been shown that those who have weak boundaries themselves tend to violate the boundaries of others.

Recognize that other people's needs and feelings are not more important than your own. Many women have traditionally thought that the needs of their husbands and children are more important than their own. This is not only untrue, but it can undermine the healthy functioning of the family dynamic. If a woman is worn out mentally and physically from putting everyone else first, she not only destroys her own health, she in turn deprives her family of being fully engaged in their lives. Instead, she should encourage every family member to contribute to the whole as well as take care of himself or herself. Putting themselves last is not something only women do, but many men as well.

Learn to say no. Many of us are people-pleasers and often put ourselves at a disadvantage by trying to accommodate everyone. We don't want to be selfish, so we put our personal needs on the back burner and agree to do things that may not be beneficial to our well-being. A certain amount of "selfishness" is necessary for having healthy personal boundaries. You do not do anyone any favors, least of all yourself, by trying to please others at your own expense.

Identify the actions and behaviors that you find unacceptable. Let others know when they've crossed the line, acted inappropriately, or disrespected you in any way. Do not be afraid to tell others when you need emotional and physical space. Allow yourself to be who you really are without pressure from others to be anything else. Know what actions you may need to take if your wishes aren't respected.

Trust and believe in yourself. You are the highest authority on you. You know yourself best. You know what you need, want, and value. Don't let anyone else make the decisions for you. Healthy boundaries make it possible for you to respect your strengths, abilities and individuality as well as those of others. An unhealthy imbalance occurs when you encourage neediness, or are needy; want to be rescued, or are the rescuer, or when you choose to play the victim. Learn to recognize when your personal boundaries are being imposed upon. Many times we try to un-ring the bell and back step on the things that are important to us.

Physical personal boundaries are the amount of space that you allow another person to enter. We tend to have a smaller circle of personal space for our friends and family, and we have a larger sphere around us when dealing with strangers. Many people are "huggers" and it is their way of being friendly and welcoming. Some people are more stand-offish and prefer a firm handshake over social kissing and hugging. Determine what you feel comfortable with and practice how you will handle someone imposing their presence in your personal space. If you prefer not to be hugged and you see one coming on – simply hold out your hand as if you were going to shake hands and take a step back. This is not being rude – it is being proactive about how you wish to be approached in a social situation.

Respecting other people's boundaries is just as important as setting your own, and they won't always be the same. Allow them their boundaries – or lack of them – and respect your differences. Always remember – you can control what is going on in your own life, but you can't control what others are doing in theirs. Let them manage their business and you manage yours. Many times, peace and forgiveness is achieved by simply agreeing to disagree. There is no harm in "peace achieved" just for the sake of peace.

Think about areas in your life where you feel like your boundaries have been violated or not respected. List those areas here:

_____
_____
_____
_____
_____
_____
_____
_____
_____
_____
_____
_____
_____
_____
_____
_____
_____
_____
_____
_____
_____
_____
_____
_____
_____
_____
_____
_____
_____

_____
_____
_____
_____
_____
_____
_____
_____
_____
_____
_____
_____
_____
_____
_____
_____
_____
_____
_____
_____
_____
_____
_____
_____
_____
_____
_____
_____
_____
_____
_____
_____

Which of those boundaries have you told other people about?

_____
_____
_____
_____
_____
_____
_____
_____

_____
_____
_____
_____
_____
_____
_____
_____
_____
_____
_____
_____

Which of those boundaries did you not tell others about?

_____
_____
_____
_____
_____
_____
_____
_____
_____
_____
_____
_____
_____
_____

What are ways you can establish and communicate these boundaries to others?

_____
_____
_____
_____
_____
_____
_____

_____
_____
_____
_____
_____
_____
_____
_____
_____

Sometimes when we are in the heat of the moment, it is difficult to think about communicating our boundaries to others. It helps if you can plan, and practice, a way to share your boundaries so you are prepared to use them when needed.

My plans for communicating my boundaries are:

_____
_____
_____
_____
_____
_____
_____
_____
_____
_____
_____
_____
_____
_____
_____
_____
_____
_____
_____
_____
_____
_____

CHAPTER 10
Money

Why is the chapter on money right after the chapter on decisions? Because managing money is an ongoing decision and one that we all need help with!

Money is at the center of most peoples' lives. We fret over it constantly – whether we have enough – worry about what it is or isn't doing. But, money isn't what's important – it's what you do with it. If you obsess about money and are a victim of overspending regularly on things that are just providing some kind of comfort to your physical well-being but will make you suffer guilt and self-loathing afterwards…you might want to consider learning a lesson about money.

One of the smartest things any one can do is to manage their own money. In an era where financial futures are so uncertain, it only makes sense to be sure you are the one who oversees your finances. We must learn to manage the money we earn wisely and plan for ourselves and our families.

Managing money is not about NOT trusting your partner – it's about trusting yourself. You must get control of your spending habits – not just hope for more money. If you manage what you have well – you will be rewarded with peace later. Gaining control over your own money will put you on a power trip that you can be proud of. It is imperative that you understand money and how you can unlock its grip on your life. It's not hard but it feel really hard when you are barely making enough to cover your bills.

Phase One - Start Saving Now!

Social Security isn't enough to live on and health care doesn't get less expensive as we get older. Saving for retirement allows you to be able to enjoy your later years.

There are three reasons to save money regularly.

1. For Retirement – Many people are retiring well after our 62-year-old parent's retirement age. Especially women. In fact – more than a third of women over the age of 50 are living below the poverty line. Social Security and even if you want to work part time or even have a money-making opportunity in retirement. The earlier you start, the better off you are.

2. For Emergencies – They happen. Just when you thought you were out of the woods and have everything all set, an unexpected expense can arise, and if you have money set aside for just such a situation – whether it be a car repair or an emergency trip to the vet for Fido – one crisis won't turn into two because you had to borrow from your rent money. The standard formula for an emergency savings fund is to have 8 months of expenses in reserve and easily accessible. Don't feel bad about not being able to achieve this right away – or even within your first year out of prison. But making a five year goal of having 3 months of living expenses in a savings account is an achievable goal.

3. For Special Events or Large Purchases – A house...a car...a wedding...a vacation? You can have them all with a little dedicated planning. Set your financial goals and make them reasonable – and celebrate their attainment. There are standardized formulas for all major purchases. Do your research, decide what your goals are, plan and stick to it. Most lenders require 20% down on a home purchase. The down payment on a car is usually about the same.

The important thing is that you start saving today. Start by saving the change in your pocket at the end of the day and sign up for an auto saving plan with your bank.

Wouldn't it be great if Prince or Princess Charming came to you with his or her own joint retirement plan? But they aren't. Not that we don't welcome them if they should manage to stumble over us while we are seeking ourselves...but one thing we are all going to agree to is to be – at the very least – aware of our finances and their status and complications.

If you have even just a month or two of bills in savings, your mind and spirit will have a peace you didn't even know existed. It doesn't happen all at once but over time. Be aware of your spending and saving habits. Make changes where you can. When we get wound up about a lack of finances, we create chaos and stress where there really is none…or at least where there could be none. Your attitude about money is as important as the money itself. Don't take it for granted, treat it with respect, and it will treat you in kind.

Phase Two – Know where your money is going!

Do you remember the earlier quote from Dave Ramsey? As a refresher, Dave Ramsey says to have a budget to tell your money where to go, instead of trying to figure out where it went!

The best way to start respecting your finances is to give yourself a 60-day reality check by keeping track of all the money you spend. Carry a notebook and track every cent or do it on your smart phone. At the end of the month calculate all the expenditures and separate them into categories. By the end of two months you will have a good idea of where you can make cuts that will allow you to save more. If you want to use a debit card and export the information from your bank statement to a spreadsheet it will even be easier to get an idea of where your money is going.

Once you know where your money is going, it's time to set up a budget to help you understand and gain control of your finances.

Phase Three – Set a plan to manage your money.

A budget is setting the maximum amount of money that you could spend during any given month plotted against the amount of money you earn during the month. As with everything, there are mathematical formulas for generating a working budget worksheet.

- Rent/Mortgage – should be no more than 25% of your total gross bring home pay. This amount should include insurance and escrow money for property taxes if you own your home.
- Savings – should be at least 10% of you monthly gross wages. Most financial planners would like to see it at 15% or even 20%. You can break the savings up for different goals or projects. You should start by accumulating your emergency

fund. Once you have 8 months of expenses saved, you can start saving for other major purchases.

- Utilities include phone, water, electricity, cable and other things that enable you to function in daily life.
- Transportation can be a car payment, insurance and gas or bus or train fare. Remember to service your vehicle regularly to prevent major repairs.
- Food includes the food you cook at home and the food and beverages you have when you are out.
- Personal/Household Expenses are makeup, skin care, clothing, household items such as furniture, cleaning supplies, and decorative items.

Find out where your money is going and make changes that will allow you to have the things you want without having empty pockets at the end of the month. Use coupons and shop sales. Look for the best deal. Reduce. Reuse. Recycle. Customize the following budget worksheet for your life.

BUDGET WORKSHEET

Weekly Expenses	Amount	x	Monthly	Seasonal Expenses	Amount	/	Monthly
Dining Out/Fast Food		2.18		Medical		3	
Groceries		2.18		Dental		3	
Dry Cleaning/Laundry		2.18		Clothing		3	
Gas for Car		2.18		Car Maintenance		3	
		2.18				3	
		2.18				3	

Monthly Expenses			Yearly Expenses		
Mortgage (PITI)/Rent	1		Registration & License	12	
Condo Fees	1		Tax Preparation	12	
Car Payment	1		Home Maintenance	12	
Garage Fees	1		Vacation/Travel	12	
Public Transportation	1		Gifts	12	
Utilities	1		Retirement	12	
Bank Fees	1		Savings	12	
Club & Union Dues	1		Education	12	
News, Magazines, Books	1			12	
Entertainment	1			12	
Household Supplies	1			12	
Personal Care	1				
Charity	1				
Court-ordered Payments	1				
Childcare	1				
Subscriptions	1				
P.O. Box	1				
Storage Unit	1				
Student Loans	1				
Credit Card Payments	1				
	1				
	1				
	1				
	1				
	1				

Did you remember coffee and hair cuts?

If your mortgage doesn't include your insurance & taxes, did you add it to the budget?

Utilities: Electric, Phone, Cable, Cell Phone, Internet, Trash Pickup, Water & Sewer, Heating Fuel, etc.

Insurance: Renter's, Homeowners, Life, Health, Disability, Car, etc.

Medical: Prescriptions, OTC Medications, Co-payments

Important: Only include expenses that aren't deducted from your paycheck.

NOTES:

CHAPTER 11
The Tough Stuff

Facing and Conquering Fear

Our Deepest Fear

Our deepest fear is not that we are inadequate.
Our deepest fear is that we are powerful beyond measure.
It is our Light, not our Darkness, that most frightens us.
We ask ourselves, who am I to be brilliant, gorgeous, talented, fabulous?
Actually, who are you NOT to be?
You are a child of God.
You're playing small does not serve the world. There is nothing enlightening about shrinking so that other people won't feel unsure around you.
We were born to make manifest the glory of God that is within us.
It is not just in some of us; it is in everyone.
As we let our own Light shine, we unconsciously give other people permission to do the same.
As we are liberated from our own fear, our presence automatically liberates others.
~ Marianne Williamson

Fear is one of the most debilitating emotions we can face. Fear of the unknown – or what could happen tomorrow – can literally stop us from accomplishing even the smallest of tasks – even when we know there is really nothing we can do about tomorrow. If we think things through logically and without the passion that fear brings with it, we often discover that what we were fearful of was the unknown.

Fear of what we don't know is perfectly natural. Many people never make positive changes in their life because they are so comfortable in their misery they can't even conceive that anything could be better…just because then it would be different. Today – consider that there is the possibility of possibility!

Healthy Person- Healthy Family.
You were created perfectly. Our bodies and our minds were meant to work together to achieve our full potential. The world that we live in created an ideal image that men and women have been trying to live up to for almost as long as we have been in existence. But all men and women are different and we each have different looks, styles, preferences and abilities. That's not the "healthy" we are talking about.

It's not about a number on a scale or our clothing size. It's about having the energy and enthusiasm for daily activities with family and friends and being able to excel at work and school activities.

If you feel good – you will look good.

All that said, there are some steps we can take to becoming healthier. Start with a balanced diet and stay away from white sugar, white flour and caffeine. These simple changes can affect your mood in a matter of days. You will be less angry and depressed and that alone will make you feel better.

1. Increase the fruits and vegetable portions of your daily eating routine and eliminate sodas – even diet sodas – as much as possible.
2. Find an activity that raises your heart rate and do it every day. You don't have to join a gym or even call it exercise…try ballroom dancing or take a karate class.
3. Get yourself on a schedule. Get up at the same time every day and go to bed at a reasonable hour. Even if you don't have anything to

do, take a shower, get dressed and ready for the day like you have somewhere to go. If you have a hard time getting to sleep or are experiencing night terrors, get into a routine of quiet time an hour before you go to bed. Avoid electronics for at least an hour before you lie down to sleep. Take a hot bubble bath, drink of cup of chamomile tea and read a book or listen to relaxing music.

4. Lastly, surround yourself with positive people...at this point, you know who they aren't – so make some new friends and build better relationships.

Forgiveness.

Everyone has been hurt by the actions or words of another. Perhaps your mother criticized your parenting skills, or your partner had an affair. These wounds can leave you with lasting feelings of anger, bitterness and even vengeance — but if you don't practice forgiveness, you may be the one who pays most dearly. By embracing forgiveness, you embrace peace, hope, gratitude and joy. By embracing anger, resentment, guilt and shame, you block any chance of moving forward.

What is forgiveness?

Generally, forgiveness is a decision to let go of resentment and thoughts of revenge. The act that hurt or offended you may always remain a part of your life, but forgiveness can lessen its grip on you and help you focus on other, positive parts of your life   Forgiveness doesn't mean that you deny the other person's responsibility for hurting you, and it doesn't minimize or justify the wrong. You can forgive the person without excusing the act. Forgiveness brings a kind of peace that helps you go on with life.

What are the benefits of forgiving someone?

Letting go of grudges and bitterness makes way for compassion, kindness and peace. Forgiveness can lead to healthier relationships, greater spiritual and psychological well-being, less stress and hostility, and fewer symptoms of depression, anxiety and chronic pain

Why is it so easy to hold a grudge?

When you're hurt by someone you love and trust, you may become angry, sad or confused. If you dwell on hurtful events or situations, grudges filled with resentment may take root. If you allow negative feelings to crowd out positive feelings, you may find yourself swallowed up by your own bitterness or sense of injustice. Bitterness can complicate the healing process – if not completely block it.

What are the effects of holding a grudge?

If you're unforgiving, you may pay the price repeatedly by bringing anger and bitterness into every relationship and new experience. Your life may become so wrapped up in the wrong you've experienced, you can't enjoy the present. You may become depressed or anxious. You may feel that your life lacks meaning or purpose or that you're at odds with your spiritual beliefs. You may lose valuable and enriching connectedness with others.

How do I reach a state of forgiveness?

Forgiveness is a commitment to a process of change. A way to begin is by recognizing the value of forgiveness and its importance in your life at a given time. Then reflect on the facts of the situation, how you've reacted, and how this combination has affected your life, health and well-being. When you're ready, actively choose to forgive the person who's offended you. Move away from your role as victim and release the control and power the offending person and situation have had in your life. As you let go of grudges, you'll no longer define your life by how you've been hurt. You may even find compassion and understanding.

What happens if I can't forgive someone?

Forgiveness can be challenging. It may be particularly hard to forgive someone who doesn't admit wrong or doesn't speak of his or her sorrow. You may want to talk with a person you've found to be wise and compassionate, such as a spiritual leader, a mental health provider, or an unbiased family member or friend. You may also want to reflect on times you've hurt others and on those who've forgiven you. Keep in mind that forgiveness has the potential to increase your sense of integrity, peace and overall well-being.

Does forgiveness guarantee reconciliation?

If the hurtful event involved someone whose relationship you otherwise value, forgiveness may lead to reconciliation. This isn't always the case, however. Reconciliation may be impossible if the offender has died or is unwilling to communicate with you. In other cases, reconciliation may not be appropriate, especially if you were attacked or assaulted. But even in those cases, forgiveness is still possible — even if reconciliation isn't.

What if I must interact with the person who hurt me, but I don't want to?

If you haven't reached a state of forgiveness, being near the person who hurt you may be tense and stressful. To handle these situations, remember that you have a choice whether to attend specific functions and gatherings. Respect yourself and do what seems best. If you choose to attend, don't be surprised by a certain amount of awkwardness and perhaps even more intense feelings. Do your best to keep an open heart and mind.

What if the person I'm forgiving doesn't change?

Getting another person to change his or her actions, behavior or words isn't the point of forgiveness. Think of forgiveness more about how it can change your life — by bringing you more peace, happiness, and emotional and spiritual healing. Forgiveness takes away the power the other person continues to wield in your life.

What if I'm the one who needs forgiveness?

Consider admitting the wrong you've done to those you've harmed, speaking of your sincere sorrow or regret, and specifically asking for forgiveness — without making excuses. Remember, however, you can't force someone to forgive you. Others need to move to forgiveness in their own time. Simply acknowledge your faults and admit your mistakes. Then commit to treating others with compassion, empathy and respect.

Seven Steps to Forgiveness

1. Select a bitter sorrow, a serious grievance against someone or a punishing charge against yourself and review in complete detail.
2. Hold in your mind the image of whatever is to be forgiven – yourself, another person or a past event – and say, "I release you from the grip of my sadness, disapproval, condemnation or despair." Quietly concentrate on this intention.

3. Imagine for a while a way your life would be without this sorrow, grievance or despair that has been haunting you.
4. Make amends with someone you have hurt or someone that has hurt you. Tell a friend about your self-forgiveness and bring your inner work to your relationships.
5. Ask for help to overcome whatever fear you have about letting go of the resentful feelings and know that help will always come.
6. Have patience. Forgiveness induces healing in its own order and timing. Whether you think you have accomplished anything so far is less important than the radical shift in your thinking about the act of forgiveness. Go about your daily business and be alert for shifts in consciousness and be ready for changes that will exceed your expectation!
7. Repeat every day for the rest of your life.

Anger Management

We all know what anger is, and we've all felt it: whether as a fleeting annoyance or as full-fledged rage. Anger is a completely normal, usually healthy, human emotion. But when it gets out of control and turns destructive, it can lead to problems — problems at work, in your personal relationships, and in the overall quality of your life. And it can make you feel as though you're at the mercy of an unpredictable and powerful emotion. This segment is meant to help you understand and control anger.

Anger is an emotional state that varies in intensity from mild irritation to intense fury and rage. Like other emotions, it is accompanied by physiological and biological changes; when you get angry, your heart rate and blood pressure go up, as do the levels of your energy hormones, adrenaline, and noradrenaline.

Anger can be caused by both external and internal events. You could be angry at a specific person (such as a coworker or supervisor) or event (a traffic jam, a canceled flight), or your anger could be caused by worrying or brooding about your personal problems. Memories of traumatic or enraging events can also trigger angry feelings.

The instinctive, natural way to express anger is to respond aggressively. Anger is a natural, adaptive response to threats; it inspires powerful, often aggressive, feelings and behaviors that allow us to fight and defend ourselves when we are attacked. A certain amount of anger, therefore, is necessary to our survival. On the other hand, we can't physically lash out at every person or object that irritates or annoys us; laws, social norms, and common-sense place limits on how far our anger can take us.

People use a variety of both conscious and unconscious processes to deal with their angry feelings. The three main approaches are expressing, suppressing, and calming. Expressing your angry feelings in an assertive— not aggressive—manner is the healthiest way to express anger. To do this, you must learn how to make clear what your needs are and how to get them met without hurting others. Being assertive doesn't mean being pushy or demanding; it means being respectful of yourself and others.

Anger can be suppressed, and then converted or redirected. This happens when you hold in your anger, stop thinking about it, and focus on something positive. The aim is to inhibit or suppress your anger and convert it into more constructive behavior. The danger in this type of response is that if it isn't allowed outward expression, your anger can turn inward—on yourself. Anger turned inward may cause hypertension, high blood pressure, or depression.

Unexpressed anger can create other problems. It can lead to pathological expressions of anger, such as passive-aggressive behavior (getting back at people indirectly, without telling them why, rather than confronting them head-on) or a personality that seems perpetually cynical and hostile. People who are constantly putting others down, criticizing everything, and making cynical comments haven't learned how to constructively express their anger. Not surprisingly, they aren't likely to have many successful relationships.

Finally, you can calm down inside. This means not just controlling your outward behavior, but also controlling your internal responses, taking steps to lower your heart rate, calm yourself down, and let the feelings subside.

The goal of anger management is to reduce both your feelings and the physiological arousal that anger causes. You can't get rid of, or avoid, the things or people that enrage you, nor can you change them, but you can learn to control your reactions.

There are psychological tests that measure the intensity of angry feelings, how prone to anger you are, and how well you handle it. But chances are good that if you do have a problem with anger, you already know it. If you find yourself acting in ways that seem out of control and frightening, you might need help finding better ways to deal with this emotion.

Some people really are more "hotheaded" than others are; they get angry more easily and more intensely than the average person does. There are also those who don't show their anger in loud spectacular ways but are chronically irritable and grumpy. Easily-angered people don't always curse and throw things; sometimes they withdraw socially, sulk, or get physically ill.

People who are easily angered generally have what some psychologists call a low tolerance for frustration, meaning simply that they feel that they should not have to be subjected to frustration, inconvenience, or annoyance. They can't take things in stride, and they're particularly infuriated if the situation seems somehow unjust: for example, being corrected for a minor mistake.

What makes people this way? Many things. One cause may be genetic or physiological. There is evidence that some children are born irritable, touchy, and easily angered, and that these signs are present from a very early age. Another may be sociocultural. Anger is often regarded as negative; we're taught that it's all right to express anxiety, depression, or other emotions but not to express anger. As a result, we don't learn how to handle it or channel it constructively.

Research has also found that family background plays a role. Typically, people who are easily angered come from families that are disruptive, chaotic, and not skilled at emotional communications.

Strategies to Keep Anger at Bay

Relaxation.
Simple relaxation tools such as deep breathing and relaxing imagery can help calm down angry feelings. There are books and courses that can teach you relaxation techniques, and once you learn the techniques, you can call upon them in any situation. If you are involved in a relationship where both partners are hot-tempered, it might be a good idea for both of you to learn these techniques.

Breathe deeply, from your diaphragm; breathing from your chest won't relax you. Picture your breath coming up from your "gut."

Slowly repeat a calm word or phrase such as "relax," "take it easy." Repeat it to yourself while breathing deeply.

Use imagery; visualize a relaxing experience from either your memory or your imagination.

Non-strenuous, slow yoga-like exercises can relax your muscles and make you feel much calmer.

Practice these techniques daily. Learn to use them automatically when you're in a tense situation.

Cognitive Restructuring.

Simply put, this means changing the way you think. Angry people tend to curse, swear, or speak in highly-colorful terms that reflect their inner thoughts. When you're angry, your thinking can get more exaggerated and overly dramatic. Try replacing these thoughts with more rational ones. For instance, instead of telling yourself, "Oh, it's awful, it's terrible, everything's ruined," tell yourself, "It's frustrating, and it's understandable that I'm upset about it, but it's not the end of the world and getting angry is not going to fix it anyhow."

Be careful of words like "never" or "always" when talking about yourself or someone else. "This !&*%@ machine never works," or "you're always forgetting things" are not just inaccurate, they also serve to make you feel that your anger is justified and that there is no way to solve the problem. They also alienate and humiliate people who might otherwise be willing to work with you on a solution.

Remind yourself that getting angry is not going to fix anything that it won't make you feel better (and may make you feel worse).

Logic defeats anger because anger, even when it's justified, can quickly become irrational. So, use cold hard logic on yourself. Remind yourself that the world is "not out to get you," you're just experiencing some of the rough spots of daily life. Do this each time you feel anger getting the best of you, and it'll help you get a more balanced perspective. Angry people tend to demand things: fairness, appreciation, agreement, or willingness to do things their way. Everyone wants these things, and we are all hurt and disappointed when we don't get them, but angry people demand them, and when their demands aren't met, their disappointment turns into anger. As part of their cognitive restructuring, angry people need to become aware of their demanding nature and translate their expectations into desires. In other words, saying, "I would like" something is healthier than saying, "I demand," or "I must have" something. When you're unable to get what you want, you will experience the normal reactions—frustration, disappointment, hurt—but not anger. Some people use this anger to avoid feeling hurt, but that doesn't mean the hurt goes away.

Problem Solving.

Sometimes, our anger and frustration are caused by very real and inescapable problems in our lives. Not all anger is misplaced and often it's a healthy, natural response to these difficulties. There is also a cultural belief that every problem has a solution, and it adds to our frustration to find out that this isn't always the case. The best attitude to bring to such a situation, then, is not to focus on finding the solution, but rather on how you handle and face the problem.

Make a plan and check your progress along the way. Resolve to give it your best, but also not to punish yourself if an answer doesn't come right away. If you can approach it with your best intentions and efforts and make a serious attempt to face it head-on, you will be less likely to lose patience and fall into all-or-nothing thinking, even if the problem does not get solved right away.

Better Communication.

Angry people tend to jump to—and act on—conclusions, and some of those conclusions can be very inaccurate. The first thing to do if you're in a heated discussion is to slow down and think through your responses. Don't say the first thing that comes into your head, but slow down and think carefully about what you want to say. At the same time, listen carefully to what the other person is saying and take your time before answering.

Listen, too, to what is underlying the anger. For instance, you like a certain amount of freedom and personal space, and your significant other wants more connection and closeness. If he or she starts complaining about your activities, don't retaliate by painting your partner as a jailer, a warden, or an albatross around your neck. It's natural to get defensive when you're criticized, but don't fight back. Instead, listen to what emotions are underlying the words: the message that this person might feel neglected and unloved. It may take a lot of patient questioning on your part, and it may require some breathing space, but don't let your anger—or a partner's—let a discussion spin out of control. Keeping your cool can keep the situation from becoming a disastrous one.

Using Humor

"Silly humor" can help defuse rage in many ways. For one thing, it can help you get a more balanced perspective. When you get angry and call someone a name or refer to them in some imaginative phrase, stop and picture what that word would literally look like. If you're at work and you think of a coworker as a "dirtbag" or a "single-cell life form," for example, picture a large bag full of dirt (or an amoeba) sitting at your colleague's desk, talking on the phone, or going to meetings. Do this whenever a name comes into your head about another person. If you can, draw a picture of what the actual thing might look like. This will take a lot of the edge off your fury; and humor can always be relied on to help unknot a tense situation.

The underlying message of highly angry people is "things oughta go my way!" Angry people tend to feel that they are morally right, that any blocking or changing of their plans is an unbearable indignity and that they should NOT have to suffer this way. Maybe other people do, but not them!

When you feel that urge, picture yourself as a god or goddess, a supreme ruler who owns the streets and stores and office space, striding alone and having your way in all situations while others defer to you. The more detail you can get into your imaginary scenes, the more chances you have to realize that maybe you are being unreasonable. You'll also realize how unimportant the things you're angry about really are. There are two cautions in using humor. First, don't try to just "laugh off" your problems; rather, use humor to help yourself face them more constructively. Second, don't give in to harsh, sarcastic humor; that's just another form of unhealthy anger expression.

Changing Your Environment.

Sometimes it's our immediate surroundings that give us cause for irritation and fury. Problems and responsibilities can weigh on you and make you feel angry at the "trap" you seem to have fallen into and all the people and things that form that trap.

Give yourself a break. Make sure you have some "personal time" scheduled for times of the day that you know are particularly stressful. One example is the working mother who has a standing rule that when she comes home from work, for the first 15 minutes, "nobody talks to Mom unless the house is on fire." After this brief quiet time, she feels better prepared to handle demands from her kids without blowing up at them.

More Tips for Easing Up on Yourself

Timing: If you and your spouse tend to fight when you discuss things at night—perhaps you're tired, or distracted, or maybe it's just habit—try changing the times when you talk about important matters, so these talks don't turn into arguments.

Avoidance: If your child's chaotic room makes you furious every time you walk by it, shut the door. Don't make yourself look at what infuriates you. Don't say, "well, my child should clean up the room, so I won't have to be angry!" That's not the point. The point is to keep yourself calm.

Finding alternatives: If your daily commute through traffic leaves you in a state of rage and frustration, give yourself a project—learn or map out a different route, one that's less congested or more scenic. Or find another alternative, such as a bus or commuter train.

If you feel that your anger is out of control and if it is having an impact on your relationships and on important parts of your life, you might consider counseling to learn how to handle it better. A psychologist or other licensed mental-health professional can work with you in developing a range of techniques for changing your thinking and your behavior.

When you talk to a prospective therapist, tell her or him that you have problems with anger that you want to work on, and ask about his or her approach to anger management. Make sure this isn't only a course of action designed to "put you in touch with your feelings and express them"—that may be precisely what your problem is.

I must work on these "tough stuff" things from this chapter::

_____
_____
_____
_____
_____
_____
_____
_____

_____
_____
_____
_____
_____
_____
_____
_____
_____
_____
_____
_____
_____
_____
_____
_____
_____
_____
_____
_____
_____
_____
_____
_____
_____
_____
_____
_____
_____
_____
_____
_____

This is my plan for dealing with these issues:

_____
_____
_____
_____
_____
_____

CHAPTER 12

Barriers To Post-Release Success

We've covered a lot of material to help you prepare and succeed once released. We also want you to *be**ware of the barriers to post-release success!*** The major ones are:

Systematic Flaws in Pre-Release Programming

Public Attitudes

- Public and political attitudes toward crime and punishment
- No public mandate for a value-added product
- Limited call for accountability of criminal justice system

Correctional Philosophy

- Lack of a universal, positive mission
- Preparation for release is often a mere afterthought
- Lack of a roadmap for consistent, long-term change and growth

Correctional Practice

- Treatment and education activities are often token and under-funded
- Inconsistent, fragmented service delivery
- Inadequate staff preparation and training
- Lack of knowledge about true needs and how to assist

Offender Reality

- Offender dysfunction and anti-social behavior
- Hostility and skepticism

No Resulting Carry Over into Community Life

A Fatal Flaw in Corrections

Since 1798, the overriding mission of adult corrections in America has been to "maintain the safe and orderly operation" of the correctional process and its web of policies and procedures. Treatment provision to offenders has been little more than a token, ancillary and an ill-funded appendage, with less than five percent of the correctional dollar applied to anything that relates to "human development."

Three years ago, the correctional industry "awoke" to the long-ignored reality that millions of men and women are exiting prison and most are failing. "Failure" is defined as "recidivism" or a return to the criminal justice system. Based on this one-dimensional measure, the nature of an ex-convict's success is defined as the mere "absence of failure." Such a primitive perspective is immediately inappropriate in real-life terms because "success" is comprised of infinitely more than can be gauged by the myopic objective of simply "not going back to prison!"

In human terms, "success" is no different for an individual addicted to drugs than for the President of General Motors. It is a process of growth and achievement linked to results valued by the individual in concert with his or her community. Such an "unfolding" springs from a mix of pro-social values supported by constructive action and an expanding sense of achievement. Therefore, any meaningful measure of post-release success should be acknowledged as a far more complex undertaking than simply not going back to prison! In this regard, a primary function of the correctional process is to enhance the client's will and ability to operate as a value-added social unit—as a whole, healthy, contributing human being.

This demands a paradigm shift from the long-standing mindset of raw human control "by any means necessary" to a product-directed philosophy and style of management consistent with promoting human development. This in turn requires a base of consistent, high quality service provision, rather than the ineffectual, haphazard farce we've called "treatment" for two centuries. What we need is a wisdom-based approach founded on creative vision, competency and, above all, the ethical determination to do right!

But why are we faced with needing to enact such core change in the way we do business? Above all because the adult correctional process is a 100% political animal. As such it operates by pandering to the lowest level of public consciousness, which subjectively interprets treatment provision to offenders as a de facto "reward for criminality." Based on this mindset, meaningful service to "criminals" is anathema, resulting in our historic reluctance to give more than lip service to the provision of effective treatment.

Catering to this subjective, punitive perspective acts in opposition to what is required to both "reduce failure" and "promote success." Far worse, it is a precipitating cause of the very "high-risk behavior" it hypocritically bemoans! The most insidious and counter-productive aspect of contemporary corrections is that it constitutes a "culture" that serves to exacerbate the anti-social perspective and behavior of its charges. As such, the correctional process itself stands as the greatest single barrier to promoting "successful re-entry." And until this wellspring of systematic alienation is acknowledged and rectified, debate over how to "enhance successful re-entry" of convicts is little more than a cruelty joke.

Why? Because "re-entry" exists downstream from years of cumulative abuses under the iron hand of the same punitive system which, while breaking its own rules with impunity, demands that incarcerated folks "cage their rage" and correct their "criminal thinking." This blatant hypocrisy must be openly addressed and resolved before there can be any hope of improvement in the product of the punishment industry.

We cannot focus on "re-entry" without taking up the matter of a "positive product." That cannot begin without coming to grips with the ramifications of cause and effect. In the end, the most valuable outcome of the re-entry debate will be the moment of truth when we openly acknowledge our double standard and adopt the same level of responsible values and conduct we so forcefully demand of adjudicated citizens with a criminal history.

Release is imminent for roughly 97% of all incarcerated citizens. The prison doors will be opening very soon, and you will be released back to the community. No matter how long you have been in prison, being released is both exciting and frightening. New sights…new smells…it can all be overwhelming.

Addiction Treatment in Prison: An Overlooked Problem (Source: Addiction.com, used with permission)

129

Did you know that 80 percent of the American prison population abuses drugs or alcohol? Statistics show that roughly 60 percent of people arrested for most crimes test positive for illicit drugs at the time of arrest, and that 50 percent of all prison and jail inmates suffer from chemical dependency and addiction. But despite these shockingly high statistics, only a very small percentage of these individuals receive addiction treatment while incarcerated.

A 2010 report from Columbus University reveals that only 10 percent of inmates who suffer from addiction are provided with treatment during their sentences. This means that those who lack access to treatment and suffer severe addictions to substances like heroin, fentanyl, and alcohol are at risk for serious health complications and death caused by withdrawal symptoms. Furthermore, these individuals are more likely to return to abusing drugs and alcohol upon release from prison and remain stuck in a life-destructing cycle of crime and addiction.

Addiction Treatment in Prison

Research shows that providing inmates with addiction treatment in prison can greatly reduce recidivism and overall crime rates and lessen the impact of incarceration costs on the economy. Increasing access to drug treatment in prison can also teach inmates how to repair and rebuild their lives, improve their physical and psychological health, and handle important responsibilities in the outside world without turning to drugs and alcohol at moments of stress.

Following is an overview of how addiction is handled in U.S. correctional facilities and how increasing access to addiction treatment in prison can improve the country and save the lives of those incarcerated for crimes committed in the name of this chronic disease.

The War on Drugs, and Its Effect on the Prison Population

The U.S. federal prison population rose by a whopping 790 percent from 1980 to 2014 — largely due in part to the War on Drugs. Today, American prisons are consistently overcrowded and endangering the lives of both inmates and correction officers on behalf of this government-led initiative to stop illicit drug use and distribution.

The Federal Bureau of Prisons reports that almost 50 percent of inmates are in federal prison for drug offenses. When combined with the percentage of immigration-related crimes, nonviolent crimes involving drugs or immigration make up nearly 55 percent of the entire country's prison population. If sentences revolving around drug offenses were eliminated or shortened, the U.S. would spend billions less on costs associated with incarceration.

Many consider the War on Drugs a failure with regard to eliminating and controlling drug abuse in the U.S. — especially since data shows that today's illicit drugs are cheaper, deadlier, and more potent than ever. Drug use rates have also increased significantly in recent years, with global use of opioids and cocaine rising by 35 percent and 27 percent respectively from 1998 to 2008.

The War on Drugs focuses on treating addiction as a crime, when in fact, addiction is a medical disorder in the form of a chronic relapsing brain disease. Failing to offer addiction treatment in prison only further contributes to rising addiction rates, overcrowded prisons, and compromised public safety.

What Options Do Addicted Inmates Currently Have?

Drug education is the most commonly-available service offered to inmates who suffer from addiction, but this service is just one component of many that make up formal addiction treatment. Those who suffer from addiction need physical and psychological therapies like detoxification and counseling to overcome addiction as a whole. More than 25 percent of state inmates and one in five federal inmates receive support-group therapy, but this therapy alone is rarely effective at helping individuals completely overcome addiction.

Research shows that less than 10 percent of inmates nationwide have access to addiction-treatment services while in prison due to factors such as inexperienced medical staff and lack of resources. Many times, medical staff lack education about substance abuse and addiction, while correctional facilities lack funding for medications and therapies proven useful at treating addiction. Though drug treatment in prison may be offered at a minimal level, the National Institute of Drug Abuse suggests that facilities use 13 principles to properly address addiction in the criminal justice system. Prisons and treatment providers are to use these principles to help inmates get clean and teach them how to stay sober and avoid relapse following release.

These principles include raising awareness that drug addiction is a brain disease that affects behavior and that treatment must be consistent and ongoing to produce stable results and behavioral changes. The principles also suggest that addiction treatments be tailored to each individual inmate based on their unique struggle with drug abuse and should target factors commonly associated with criminal behavior. As a whole, these principles are intended to reduce recidivism rates and improve inmates' overall quality of life after overcoming addiction and leaving prison.

How Does Drug Treatment in Prison Improve Public Safety?

Since addiction is a chronic relapsing brain disease, this condition cannot go away on its own without proper treatment. Addiction treatment in prison is often overlooked on behalf of the stigma surrounding addiction — many assume that inmates will learn from their mistakes while behind bars and after having suffered painful and life-threatening withdrawal symptoms. But research shows that individuals are more likely to relapse later down the road without addiction treatment — especially inmates who return to their former lives upon release from prison.

A review of recidivism rates across 15 states revealed that 25 percent of inmates released from prison were sent back to prison within three years — many of whom tested positive for drug use at the time of arrest. But research shows that inmates who receive addiction treatment while in prison and following their release are seven times more likely to remain drug-free, and three times less likely to engage in criminal behavior than inmates who do not receive addiction treatment.

Participating in prison addiction treatment allows inmates to overcome this brain disorder that may have led to their incarceration in the first place. Inmates can first overcome chemical dependency so they no longer crave or physically rely on drugs and alcohol to function normally. Next, inmates can benefit from therapies like behavioral counseling and relapse prevention education to overcome co-occurring disorders driving their addiction and to learn the skills needed to stay sober for life after leaving prison.

Addiction treatment helps former inmates re-enter society and rebuild their lives without being distracted by drugs and alcohol. These individuals often face higher success rates in terms of employment and no longer have to suffer health problems and poor memory brought on by substance abuse. As these former inmates navigate society drug-free and without impulses to commit crimes that fuel an addiction, families and communities nationwide can benefit from improved public safety.

Treating Heroin and Painkiller Addiction in Prison
As the U.S. continues to fight its nationwide opioid epidemic outside prison walls, a high number of inmates are suffering severe cases of heroin and painkiller withdrawal behind bars — some of which have resulted in death. While heroin and painkiller withdrawal symptoms are generally not known to be life-threatening, there were four cases of jail deaths in 2015 caused by opioid withdrawal symptoms. One of those inmates died in jail before they were able to see the judge regarding the crime for which they had been arrested.

Opioid addiction in prison is commonly treated using methadone or buprenorphine — medications that help individuals safely and fully overcome heroin and painkiller dependence without suffering withdrawal symptoms. However, a recent study reveals that only 50 percent of all state and federal prisons offer medication-assisted treatment and only under limited circumstances. For instance, some prisons only offer these treatments to pregnant women or to those also suffering chronic pain from confirmed medical conditions.

When questioned about why opioid addiction treatments are so limited, jails and prisons claim that methadone and buprenorphine raise a number of security concerns and that they prefer allowing inmates to detox naturally without the use of medications. Shockingly, 50 percent of prison medical directors are unaware of the benefits of treating opioid addiction using buprenorphine, while 27 percent claim being unaware of the benefits of methadone maintenance therapy.

A controlled medical trial conducted at Rikers Island Jail in New York showed that inmates treated with buprenorphine are more likely to stick with addiction treatment throughout incarceration and produce higher attendance rates at continuing-care programs after their release. Another study shows that inmates who receive methadone and counseling in prison are more likely to stay clean one year following release than inmates who only receive counseling. Evidence backs up the efficacy of opioid-addiction treatment and its role in helping former inmates stay clean and avoiding relapse following their prison sentences.

How Should Prisons Handle Drug Addiction?

At present, the U.S. government spends over 95 percent of funds allocated for substance abuse and addiction on the consequences brought on by drug abuse, such as hospitalization and incarceration. The remaining percentage of funds are spent on addiction prevention and treatment — meaning the country is wasting billions by being reactive instead of proactive with regard to addressing the nation's drug problem. Data shows that the U.S. can earn over $90,000 per year for every inmate who receives addiction treatment, which would otherwise be spent on unemployment, incarceration, and related costs driven by lack of drug treatment in prison.

Based on the NDA's principles of drug-abuse treatments for prison systems, the most effective ways to treat addiction involve evaluating inmates for underlying mental health disorders and offering consistent treatment from trained medical staff who can administer medication-assisted therapies. Additionally, correctional facilities can implement long-term programs that involve supporting inmates in their communities following release from prison.

While these solutions may seem costly for state and federal governments, the benefits far outweigh the costs. Today, the addiction treatments available across prisons vary depending on the facility and its resources. A study conducted by the National Center on Addiction and Substance Abuse found that only 65 percent of correctional facilities offer individual or group counseling in the form of cognitive-behavioral therapy, behavioral counseling, and similar therapies. Self-help groups such as Alcoholics Anonymous and Narcotics Anonymous are available at 74 percent of prisons and serve as useful interventions that encourage a supportive environment among those in recovery.

What Steps Can You Take to Help?

Many times, addiction begins at home and can be triggered by a wide range of risk factors including family genetics, environment, and mental health disorders. Addressing substance abuse and addiction at its earliest stages allows you and your loved ones to stay in control of your lives and avoid turning to crime and unlawful behavior for the sake of obtaining and using drugs and alcohol. Familiarize yourself with common signs of addiction and intervene at the right time so your loved one can receive addiction treatment as needed.

Americans can acknowledge and address the stigma surrounding addiction and former inmates and help communities understand that addiction is a brain disease—not a form of criminal behavior. Drugs can alter the way the brain functions and influence its victims to continue using drugs and alcohol despite negative consequences. Many times, those who suffer from addiction commit crimes so they can afford and obtain drugs and so they can avoid experiencing severe withdrawal symptoms associated with drug abuse.

The presence of mental-health disorders can also increase one's risk for addiction. Individuals who suffer from depression, bipolar disorder, and anxiety disorders like OCD may use drugs and alcohol to self-medicate and avoid symptoms associated with their disorders. If a friend or loved one suffers a mental-health disorder, look for signs that may indicate drug abuse so your loved one can be treated for both conditions at a nearby drug rehabilitation center.

According to Addiction.com, nearly 80% of all incarcerated citizens have struggled with drug addiction, alcohol abuse, or both. Clearly, not dealing with underlying addictions is a dangerous trap that contributes to the dismally high recidivism rate we suffer with in our country.

Here are important tips from addiction.com to help you deal with addictions.

1. Start visualizing/thinking about coming back.

"Really spend some time thinking through every step of leaving prison—not just the fun parts, like eating your Mom's fried chicken. Spend some serious time walking, almost minute by minute, through what you will do the day you leave, how you will leave, etc."

"If you are in recovery, think about what could trigger you to pick up again. Despite your best intentions, before you know it, you'll end up in your old copping spots. Think about parts of the city that you should avoid for a while." The Big Book talks about "people, places and things," and it's real easy to slide back into something that will get you back inside.

Professional athletes are trained to visualize every second of a particular goal or game. They break down their movements, breathing, etc. Going through it time after time keeps a distraction (or their nerves) from tripping them up. Things to include are: going to see your parole officer, finding a case manager to help with an apartment and entitlements, and avoiding people who may try to pull you down. Really let yourself get into the moment—see what you will see, smell what you will smell, and hear what you will hear, etc.

2. Build flexibility into your visualization.
When you get back, things may be different than you pictured them—you may have to do things in a different order or people may treat you differently. Don't let that throw you. Be thinking "If A happens, then I'll do .... But if B happens instead, this is how I'll handle it." Remember "When Life Hands You Lemons, Make Lemonade."

3. Frustration is part of the process—be ready for it.
If you are returning to where you used to use drugs, you will be coming back to one of the most challenging places in the world. There are millions of people, and it often seems that they all want what you want—and are in front of you in line. Workers will be rude to you, lose your paperwork, tell you to come back tomorrow, and won't be in the office when you need them to be there. This can make you feel dumb, stupid, and angry or a whole mixture of emotions. This is normal. Frustration is part of life for every person living, not just those coming back from prison. Figuring out a good way to respond when all you want to do is yell at someone or rip the door off the wall is vital.

4. Drug use.
If you are still using, it is very important to avoid getting additional strains of HIV that are resistant to the new drugs. Get in touch with the local needle exchanges, get your own works and don't share. If you must share, clean with bleach and get your own set as soon as possible. Think seriously about quitting—a drug-related arrest can send you back to prison.

If you are working a system of recovery, make a meeting as soon as possible and share in the meeting. Get a local sponsor if you don't have one. Be on the alert for relapse triggers—drugs and alcohol will be ready to trip you up at every opportunity.

Twelve-stepping can be a good way to get support and help to resist the urge to pick up. Your sponsor or home group is likely to suggest "90 in 90" which means making 90 meetings in 90 days, or one a day for the first three months. Every meeting has its own character, and if you dislike one, go to another at a different location or time. Meetings are held literally around the clock, in all sorts of places, in many different locations throughout New York. Staying sober can be one of the most important things you do to stay out of prison.

5. Be ready to be overwhelmed with the options.

When you were in prison, you may have had only a few choices to make each day—most of them were made for you. But in the community, just the sheer number of choices can cause you to feel stunned. Get an apartment, a job, go to school, on a date, buy a car, visit friends, there are many, many choices to make. You will feel overwhelmed, and that's okay—the important thing is not to feel rushed into a bad decision or stay in bed all day to avoid making any decisions at all.

6. Life is faster outside prison.

Maria said, "When I got out, everything was moving so fast that one day I grabbed onto a lamppost to make it slow down." You will be expected to make decisions, go places, and show up, etc. the same day or in a matter of hours. Most people adjust fairly quickly, while others take a little more time to get used to the faster pace when there are more choices available.

7. Take things one step at a time.

When you first get out, you will have a lot of things to get organized and you'll have to decide what to tackle first. For example, you may decide to get your entitlements lined up before you hit the job market. In order to get your benefits, you will need a case manager who can help get all the paperwork together and filed for you. And so your first priority becomes getting a case manager. Don't try to get a job, case manager, apartment, relationship, your kids back, enroll in school and buy a car all in the same week.

Shandra said: "When I got out of Bedford Hills, I moved to my sister's couch, got a job but then found out that since I slept in the living room, I went to bed last. I was always late for work and got fired. I should have waited on the job until I had a good place to sleep or taken a second-shift job so I could sleep after the kids left for school."

8. Usually parole won't come down hard if you don't get a job immediately.
They've seen a lot of people come out (and go back to) prison. Often their perspective is that if you are working closely with a case manager, you are working on staying out. Your parole officer will want updates on what tasks or entitlements you are working on, what support groups you're going to, etc. He or she wants to see activities in your schedule that are aimed at you staying out of prison. Getting a job will be one of these, but many P.O.s know it is best if you get settled first.

9. Seek assistance.
You are engaged in a difficult process, and with all large jobs, you will need help to successfully accomplish it. Successful athletes rely on whole teams of experts—from the people who design their shoes and equipment to trainers, coaches, and advisers. This is a bigger challenge—talk to transitional planners, find people outside who have successfully returned, and involve yourself with the agencies and resources that can help. They have helped literally hundreds of thousands of people in the community— why deny yourself all that knowledge?

10. Respect the advice of professionals.
You don't have to act on it or accept it blindly. Respecting it will smooth your way. You may think only someone who has been in your shoes can give worthwhile advice. But that person can only offer you their experience. A transitional planner or case manager may have helped thousands of people successfully return from prison even if the case manager never served time themselves. They can give you the lessons they learned from seeing so many people succeed.

11. What seems desperate to you may not be to someone else.
Don't assume that just because the worker or case manager isn't looking upset, that they aren't going to help you, or they don't understand. They might be waiting for you to finish talking before telling you where to get the

help you need. Sometimes they know that what you need and it might take some time to apply for or find.

12. Getting angry and creating a scene will not always achieve your goals, it could even make it harder.

Assume that you'll have to wait most places you'll seek help. Keep in mind that some of the things you'll need can only be supplied by one or two agencies. Politely ask how soon you can be seen. Remember when you were inside? People who annoy prison guards wait longer for anything they want. If you yell at someone or create a scene, they might help you that one time right away and then bar you from ever getting help at that agency again. Or they might just throw you out.

Feel ignored? Feel your needs aren't being taken seriously? Hold on to anger as your last weapon, because once you've used it, you may not be able to go back to that agency again. Don't burn bridges before you even get to them.

13. Agencies and staff are busy.

You are not the only one who needs help. Sometimes this is easy to see, especially if there are a lot of people in the waiting room. Other times you may be the only one waiting, but the staff is always answering the phones or writing stuff down and not dealing with you. Non-profit agencies run on very little money and limited staff. The best have lots of clients needing help. Politely ask the receptionist when she or he thinks you'll be seen. Sometimes they know, but often they have no way of knowing. Always come with a book, a friend or something to do while you wait.

14. If you are truly in need, don't let barriers keep you from getting what you need to survive.

If you are hungry, don't have a winter coat or shoes, don't have the medications you need, or don't have a place to sleep, get help. These needs are what social service agencies deal with daily. Even if you are dirty, smell, have been sleeping in the subway, or are coming off a drug run, etc., call the Osborne Association at (718) 842-0500. The most important thing is to survive—if you are alive, you can get help to rebuild your life.

15. Don't decide too fast something isn't working out.
Tony said:

> When I left Riker's, DASIS put me in an SRO in Queens. I've only lived in Manhattan and I got lost finding it. I had six months sober, the manager sold crack, and every night was party time. I went to my case manager early the next morning. He said I could have better housing in six months or I could go to the shelters. I stayed, and in six months I got a shot at a clean, sunny, apartment to share with one guy, but in Staten Island! I took it and saved enough in a year to move to Manhattan. Looking back if I'd gone into the shelters, I would have ended up strung out and probably back inside."

16. Everything about you is not in the computer.
There is no central file in the computer with everything about you. DOCS, Medicaid, and your doctor all have separate files in their computers, but their computer systems are not linked together, and each has information that they can't share with the others. Ordinary people who have a computer can't access information about you from DOCS, Medicaid, etc. These are all private systems and aren't shared with the public.

17. Keep an appointment book.
Pocket-sized books can be purchased cheaply at newsstands and stationary stores. You will have many appointments to remember—it will be impossible to keep them all in your head.

18. Keep appointments when they are made.
Want a way to make yourself remembered among all the others waiting for services, applying for jobs, etc.? Show up on time for appointments. Can't be there on time or have to cancel? Call to notify the person you were scheduled to see. Appointments are a way to honor YOUR time— otherwise agencies would make you wait hours and hours. At your parole office and for job interviews, appointment times are tests to see if you are serious about following through.

19. Show up as neat and clean as possible.
If you can, shave, shower and wear clean clothes. At the very least, wash your face and hands and comb your hair. Staff of agencies have seen people

living in desperate circumstances, but they will be more likely to help you if you are at least trying to make a better appearance.

Malcolm X (who successfully rebuilt his life after prison) said "by any means necessary." If there is a person, support group, tip, hint, etc. that can help you get out and stay out, grab it and use it. The rest of your life is waiting to happen.

I can identify with the following Barriers to Post-Release Success:

_____
_____
_____
_____
_____
_____
_____
_____
_____

My plan to deal with these barriers is:

_____
_____
_____
_____
_____
_____
_____
_____
_____

I must deal with the following addictions to be successful in post-release:

_____
_____
_____
_____
_____

My plan for dealing with these addictions is:

_____
_____
_____

CHAPTER 13
Charm School
(Manners for the Real World)

Why do manners matter? Like John Maxwell says: the whole world, with one notable exception, is made up of others. No matter how much you may try to avoid it, if we are alive, we have to deal with others. Why not interact with them in a way that makes our own lives better, or easier?

There are five elements to expressing excellent etiquette in today's world, and they have nothing to do with which fork to use. They are:

Respect
Consideration
Honesty
Graciousness
Deference

Courteous behavior is a result of a courteous mindset. The rules of courteous behavior have changed with the times but the idealism behind them remains the same.

There is only one single rule for every situation and that is to always treat others as you would want to be treated.

Actions express attitude and people who pay attention to others will have little trouble understanding courteous behavior. A self-centered person might say that they understand how someone else feels, but they immediately start describing their own experiences. An empathetic person would be more likely to say that they can understand the emotion the person is expressing and allow themselves to listen to what the other person is saying about how they feel.

Good manners are a necessary part of being in society, and having the ability to properly engage is social situations sets the stage for a happy life. You will be better prepared for going to work or school and have the confidence to deal with bosses, co-workers, professors and other students.

Greeting People

A greeting is a formal or informal way of acknowledging another person's presence. It can be done sitting or standing and with or without a handshake. It is a general rule to rise when someone enters the room or approaches you. There are two reasons why this is an excellent habit to adopt.

1. You will be meeting the new person at eye level which not only shows respect for the person who is entering but also keeps you from feeling intimidated by someone towering over you while introducing themselves.

2. You can extend your hand in greeting which clearly sets your space boundaries and reduces the approaching person's inclination to hug or kiss you. There is nothing wrong with hugging or air kissing someone you already know, and the accepted rule of thumb is to hug and then air kiss by leaning your cheek to the right and then – in the European fashion – to quickly lean your cheek to the left and then step back.

A handshake symbolizes both welcome and good faith and a firm grip is appreciated but should not be either limp or bone crushing. The shaking should be perceptible but not hand pumping. Release your hold after a few seconds. If you extend your hand and the other person doesn't respond, simply assume they did not see your gesture and lower your hand.

Be careful not to inconvenience someone who might be carrying things in both hands or might have an injury or infirmity that keeps them from shaking hands.

Saying "Goodbye" is necessary as well and can consist of some pleasantry that winds the conversation down such as "It's been so good to see you…" or "I wish I had more time to visit but I'll call you next week…"

Building a Wardrobe.

Building a wardrobe for work, school, home and church is fun, and there is lots of room for personal style in each of the different categories, but choosing the basics is the most important part.

A great wardrobe starts with black skirts and pants and white shirts, both button down and pull over t-shirt types. There is literally nothing that doesn't look good with black pants or a skirt, and black and white is a perfect color combination for almost any occasion. A black knee length skirt, a longer version and a cocktail length (no more than 4 inches above the knee) will get you into and out of nearly everywhere. For these basic pieces, buy quality rather than quantity. On a day when you can't decide what to wear, it's not hard to pull out these time-honored faithful's and know you will look great even on the days you don't think you care.

Everyone should have at least one good pair of black shoes. If you wear heels, it should be a low to medium one. You can experiment with different heights later – start with something reasonable. A good pair of flats can also go with jeans or shorts, and try to keep one pair of shoes on hand for when the pedicure isn't up to par.

Practice good manners and good behavior even when no one is looking, and you will never have to worry about doing the wrong thing in a social situation. Look around at the positive people in your life and find a role model – or better yet – several of them – to emulate.

Top Ten Social Graces

1. Be Grateful – Nothing will take you further than a sincere "Thank You". Saying "Please" sincerely and without whining is of equal value and demonstrates gratefulness in its own way.

2. Cell Phones should never be answered in the presence of another person. Checking your email and texting—unless you are curing cancer or splitting the atom—while having a conversation is rude.

3. An open mouth while eating just shouldn't happen...EVER! If you have something to say, chew your food and swallow before engaging in conversation.

4. Bragging or boasting is never necessary for a person who is confident in their accomplishments. The only time that self-promotion is permitted is during a job interview or when asked directly.

5. Giving and receiving of compliments should always be sincere and gracious. If someone comments on your appearance or on the preparation of a meal or regarding something you've done, simply say "Thank You."

6. Bad Breath and/or Body Odor is one of the quickest ways to ostracize yourself from pretty much everyone. Good hygiene includes brushing teeth and using mouth wash, showering or bathing as needed, using a good deodorant and never wearing too much perfume of cologne.

7. Do not use poor grammar or foul language when speaking, whether it is in public or in private. Be yourself, just don't be crude or rude.

8. Do not interrupt someone when they are speaking or cut in front of someone who you think is going too slowly. This also includes finishing other people's sentences or walking away when someone is speaking to you.

9. Gossiping is a dreadful habit and very difficult to break. Never talk about someone behind their back unless you wouldn't mind having the entire conversation played back to them verbatim with you present.

10. Be a person of your word. Blowing off appointments will quickly earn you persona-non-grata status in any social circle. No showing for an appointment—whether it be a salon appointment, a doctor's

office, or even lunch with a friend—is even worse, so don't wait
until the last minute before you make arrangements to cancel and
reschedule.

Which social graces are you best at?

_____
_____
_____

Which social graces do you need to improve?

_____
_____
_____

What steps can you take to make improvement in these areas?

_____
_____
_____

Notes:

_____
_____
_____
_____
_____
_____
_____
_____
_____
_____
_____
_____
_____
_____
_____
_____
_____
_____
_____
_____
_____

CHAPTER 14
Connecting With The Community

In our modern world there are two types of community. We most often relate to the physical community we live in, but as social media grows, the online community plays a bigger role.

There are no simple checklists for thriving in a community, except maybe the Golden Rule: Do unto others as you want them to do unto you. Hopefully the tips and lessons in this Guide have helped you develop tools you can use to make your experience in your physical and online communities better.

Let's start with the first step in reentering the physical community: rebuilding relationships.

Rebuilding Relationships

For most people reentering their community, it will take some time to get used to life back at home. You may not feel comfortable right away, and you and your family and friends may have to make some changes. Your family members will have attempted to adapt to everyday routines without you there and may have learned to do things around the house (budgeting, grocery shopping, car repair, and other household chores) that you used to do.

It is important to talk to your family about how you are feeling and decide how to take care of these things now that you are home.

Here are some other suggestions that can help:

1. Begin by appreciating the small things others take for granted – such as privacy, being able to come and go as you please, planning your meals, and more.
2. Avoid talking about life in prison as your only conversation topic.
3. Practice making "small talk" about daily events instead. It will be difficult to catch up on everything that happened while you were away.
4. Be patient with yourself and your family and friends.
5. Understand that things will take time, for both you and those around you, and that even small steps are important.
6. Trust takes time to rebuild. As your family learns to trust you, they will do so more and more, and you will begin to feel more comfortable within your family again.

Since you were in prison, a divorce or child custody proceeding may have happened and changed your family. Show your loved ones that you understand you may have hurt them and allow them to share painful memories with you.

Children may have become used to living without their mom or dad. They may not understand everything that has happened, where you were, or why you were away. You can ask them if they have any questions, and be patient with them as they readjust.

Your parents and your children are not the same as when you left - do not try to treat them the way you did. They have aged and changed. Show them you care about their needs, are interested in what they are doing, and you want to spend time with them.

If you are asked about your incarceration, answer questions honestly. You do not need to tell them it was "no big deal" or act "tough." Let them know being in prison is no way to spend your life. Take responsibility, use the Elevator Pitch for Criminal history to tell your story. Be yourself, and don't feel rejected if people don't immediately understand or embrace you.

Toxic Relationships

"When you have been really ill emotionally, you don't even know a snake when you see one. When recovery begins, you see a snake and you know it's a snake, but you still play with it. Once you have truly landed in a recovery zone, you see a snake, you know it's a snake and you cross to the other side of the road."

- *Marianne Williamson*

A toxic relationship is an addiction to anything or anyone that doesn't promote your own well-being. You can have a toxic relationship with a substance—like alcohol, food or drugs—or an activity like over-spending, compulsive behaviors like not paying your bills on time even when you have the money or constantly being late to arrive for work, school or other events. Toxic relationships require diligent attention and the support of good friends, family members and co-workers to help you conquer their power over your life.

People can also be toxic to your growth. They don't understand that you are looking into the future and are no longer bound by your past. They might look for ways to keep you at their level—to block your blessings and to blind you to the goals you have set for yourself. Regardless of who they are, you must understand that they—and others who will come along that are like them—simply have to be eliminated from your life.

Family relationships are often toxic and have to be managed differently. Limit your contact with the "crazy-makers" you are related to and pray that your life will be a beacon of hope for them to find their own way. As they see that you are committed to your own best interests, they will be powerless over you.

Identify the toxic relationships that you have faced in the past and detail their characteristics so that when they knock on the door of your future, you know not to let them in. If they don't fit the criteria of the boundaries that you have decided to set for yourself and your life, they don't have a place at your table.

These are the toxic relationships I need to avoid: _____

_____

_____

This is how I will avoid them: _____
_____
_____

If you've been incarcerated for a while, the end of this chapter will help give you a crash course in setting up a free email account, what social media is, and how to manage it/be involved with social media. Let's start with a free email account for you.

Free Gmail account

Setting up a Gmail account is easy. You will begin by creating a Google account, and during the quick signup process, you will choose your Gmail account name. In this lesson, we'll show you how to **set up** your **Google account for Gmail**, add and edit **contacts**, and edit your **mail settings**.

To create a **Gmail** address, you'll first need to create a **Google account**. Gmail will redirect you to the Google account signup page. You'll need to provide some basic information like your **name, birth date, gender**, and **location**. You will also need to choose a **name** for your new Gmail address. Once you create an account, you'll be able to start adding **contacts** and adjusting your **mail settings**.

Note: when you create your new email address, you want to make it look professional rather than something like: 2sexy2bforgotten@gmail.com. If you are applying for jobs, the sample email address above will most likely not be taken as seriously as one that includes only your name. Many people use their first and last names combined or one or the other with a number they can easily remember.

To create an account:
1. Go to www.gmail.com.
2. Click **Create account.**
3. The **signup** form will appear. Follow the directions and enter the required information.
4. Review Google's Terms of Service and Privacy Policy, click the check box, then click **Next step.**
5. Here, you'll have an opportunity to set up **recovery options**. Recovery options are helpful if you forget your password or if

someone tries to access your account. If you don't want to set up recovery options at this time, click **Done**.

6. Your account will be created, and the Google welcome page will appear.

Just like with any online service, it's important to choose a strong password. In other words, one that is difficult for someone else to guess. For more information, check out this link which gives great advice on creating strong passwords: gcflearnfree.org/internetsafety/creating-strong-passwords/1

Signing in to your account.
When you first create your account, you will be automatically signed in. Most of the time, however, you'll need to **sign in** to your account and **sign out** when you're done with it. Signing out is especially important if you're using a shared computer (for example, at a **library** or **office**) because it prevents others from viewing your emails.

To sign in:
1. Go to www.gmail.com.
2. Type your **user name** (your email address) and **password**, then click **Sign in**.

To sign out: In the top-right corner of the page, locate the circle that has your first initial (if you've already selected an avatar image, it will show the image instead). To sign out, click the circle and select **Sign out**.

Mail settings.
Occasionally, you may want to adjust Gmail's **appearance** or **behavior**. For example, you could create a **signature** or **vacation reply**, edit your **labels**, or change the **theme**. These adjustments can be made from your **mail settings**.

To access your mail settings:
1. Click the **gear icon** in the top-right corner of the page, then select **Settings**.
2. From here, you can click any of the **categories** at the top to edit the desired settings.

Adding contacts.

Like all major email providers, Gmail lets you keep an address book of **contacts** so you don't have to memorize everyone's email addresses. You can also add other contact information like **phone numbers**, **birthdays**, and **physical addresses**.

To add a contact:

1. In the **Gmail drop-down menu**, select **Contacts**.
2. Your contacts screen will appear. Click **Add new contact.**
3. Type the person's **name** or **email address**. If they have a Google+ profile, it may appear below. Click **Create** to add the contact.
4. You can also type additional contact information if desired. All changes you make will be **saved automatically**.

To edit a contact:

1. In the **Gmail drop-down menu**, select **Contacts**.
2. Click the contact you want to edit.
3. You can now make any **changes** you want to the contact.

By default, when you send an email to a new address, Gmail adds the address to your contacts. You can then go to your contacts to **edit** the person's information as needed.

Importing mail and contacts.

You may already have a contact list from another email address, and it would be a lot of work to re-enter all this information manually. Gmail allows you to import your contacts from another email account, and you can even import all your email messages from that account. Several email providers are supported, including **Yahoo!**, **Hotmail**, and **AOL**.

To add other accounts:

1. Click the gear icon in the top-right corner of the page, then select **Settings**.
2. Go to **Accounts** and click **Add a POP3 mail account you own**. You can then follow the instructions on the screen to import your mail.

Challenge!
1. If you do not already have a Gmail account, **create** one.
2. **Open** Gmail.
3. **Navigate** to your Gmail settings.
4. **Set your preferences** in your Gmail settings.
5. Add a **new contact**. You can either add one you already know, or if you'd like you can create one with the following information:
   Name: Julia Fillory
   Email: jfillory@gmail.com

Social Media

Facebook

Since its launch in 2004, Facebook has become one of the most popular social networking sites on the Internet. While many of its users are teenagers and young adults, it's also an excellent way for family members to keep in touch in our busy and often geographically-dispersed lives. Here are some suggestions on how you can get connected on Facebook.

Be open-minded. It doesn't matter what age you are—you can learn technology. The real barrier is likely to be attitude—if the younger generations believe there is no point in teaching older generations Facebook, in turn, the elderly generations may also believe there is no point being a part of such online social networking.

- Focus on the reality that many people care deeply about any method of communication that will enable them to remain connected with their family, friends, and other people they care about. The convenience, accessibility, and low expense of online interaction provides adequate motivation to try something new like Facebook, provided you explain the purpose and benefits adequately.
- Focus on making it clear that there is nothing magical or strange about Facebook. Have clear explanations ready.
- Bear in mind that adults tend to be persistent, patient, and enjoy seeking out intellectual stimulation. In addition, adults tend to be just as curious as kids. Take these positive traits and apply them to your Facebook training.

Here are some reasons to connect on Facebook:

- "It's a great way to find old buddies!"—Many people are reconnecting with long-lost friends via Facebook.
- It's a great way to meet new people and engage with people who have similar interests.
- "It's a way that you can keep in touch with me and the rest of the family!"—So, you can tap into and be aware as family grows, travels, achieves successes, etc.
- "You don't need to remember anyone's email, let alone email them!" — "You can get free deals, specials, etc., from your favorite stores and companies!" — "You can play games on Facebook!" Growing numbers of people are enjoying Facebook games, which has the added benefit of exercising the brain and hand muscles.
- "Facebook can narrow the generation gap and create a sense of community.

If you don't have a Facebook account, you can create one in a few steps:
1. Go to www.facebook.com.
2. If you see the signup form, fill out your name, email address or phone number, password, birthday and gender. If you don't see the form, click Sign Up, then fill out the form.
3. Click Sign Up.

Once you sign up, you'll need to confirm your email or phone number. If you already have a Facebook account, you can log into your account by entering your email or mobile number and password and clicking Log In. You must be at least 13 years old to sign up for Facebook.

Twitter

Let's say for a moment that you have met a very special person. They appear normal, just like you, in fact. So, what makes them so special, so out of the ordinary? You have just met the one person on Earth who doesn't know what Twitter is. That's right...the social media site your grandmother is using is a total mystery to this one, astonishing individual.

Once you have gotten up off the ground and been attended to by a paramedic who assures you that you don't have a concussion, what do you say? Think about it: how do you really explain adequately a service we all use every day? It isn't as simple as you might think.

Now, we are going to step into a first-person perspective here and try to explain to this theoretical time traveler/alien what Twitter is. Ready? Here we go:

That was a joke, right? No? Wow...alright. Well, Twitter is this social media site that...what's that? What is social media? This is going to be harder than I thought. Let's start from the beginning.

A social media site is a place where people go to share information, views and just communicate through the web. You can show them interesting or funny links, embed videos, post pictures or just talk through your status box. You can also comment on other people's posts, or join special groups dedicated to things that are important to you.

There are different kinds of social media sites. You have Facebook, which is a multipurpose site centered more around direct communication with people you really know. Then there is YouTube, where you share videos. Or Pinterest, where you put photos on a digital pin board to collect or share with others.

Twitter is yet another site. Only this one is for shorter blurbs of information. The updates only allow 140 characters, so you must be brief. This forces you to be more careful with your words, and to present only the most important information.

It is also a public format. While you can choose to make your Twitter private, most choose not to. Therefore, you are writing updates the entire world can see if they happen upon your profile. It is a great way to meet new people, find others interested in what you are, or just find something that makes you laugh or elicits reaction.

If you really enjoy something someone says, you can 'retweet it'. Which means you repost it with full credit using a simple button. If you really like someone and want to keep up with them regularly, you 'follow' them. This gives you live updates on your feed page so you can see every time they post.

How do you find people? That is the most interesting part about Twitter. Back when it was first created, in 2007, people had some problems. It used a unique search algorithm, and with its format and the nature of its public sharing, it made it hard to find and create groups. There was no way to do it without completely changing the way the site worked.

A developer working for the site named Chris Messina came up with a way to get around this. He made hashtags, which use the '#' symbol before a keyword. This creates an active link that groups together all posts with the same hashtag in a post.

Let's say, for example, you wanted to lose weight. So, you are finding others who also want to do that on Twitter for tips, inspiration and support. You could do a search for #fitness, #weightloss, #diet, #exercise or other relevant terms to find people. You could also put them in your own posts, so others could find you. In the end, this is referred to as microblogging. It is also a form of quickfire communication and very mobile friendly. That is what Twitter is.

Now, join us in the modern century and get one, will you?

Notes:

_____
_____
_____
_____
_____
_____
_____
_____
_____
_____
_____
_____
_____
_____
_____
_____
_____
_____
_____
_____
_____
_____
_____
_____
_____
_____
_____
_____
_____
_____
_____
_____
_____

CHAPTER 15

Being on Probation or Parole

Probation refers to adult offenders whom courts place on supervision in the community through a probation agency, generally in place of incarceration. However, some jurisdictions do sentence probationers to a combined short-term incarceration sentence immediately followed by probation, which is referred to as a split sentence.

Probations can have several different supervision statuses including active supervision, which means the individual is required to regularly report to a probation authority in person, by mail, or by telephone. Some probationers may be on an inactive status which means they are excluded from regularly reporting and can be due to a number of reasons. For instance, some probationers may be placed on inactive status immediately because the severity of the offense was minimal, or some may receive a reduction in supervision and therefore may be moved from an active to inactive status.

Other supervision statuses include probationers who only have financial conditions remaining, have absconded, or who have active warrants. In many instances, while on probation, offenders are required to fulfill certain conditions of their supervision (e.g., payment of fines, fees or court costs or participation in treatment programs) and adhere to specific rules of conduct while in the community. Failure to comply with any conditions can result in incarceration.

Parole refers to criminal offenders who are conditionally released from prison to serve the remaining portion of their sentence in the community. Prisoners may be released to parole either by a parole board decision (discretionary release/discretionary parole) or according to provisions of a statute (mandatory release/mandatory parole). This definition of parole is not restricted to only prisoners who are released through a parole board decision, but also includes prisoners who are released based on provisions of a statute.

Parolees can have many different supervision statuses including active supervision, which means they are required to regularly report to a parole authority in person, by mail, or by telephone. Some parolees may be on an inactive status, which means they are excluded from regularly reporting, and that could be for many reasons. For instance, some may receive a reduction in supervision, possibly due to compliance or meeting all required conditions before the parole sentence terminates, and therefore may be moved from an active to inactive status.

Other supervision statues include parolees who only have financial conditions remaining, have absconded, or who have active warrants. Parolees are also typically required to fulfill certain conditions and adhere to specific rules of conduct while in the community. Failure to comply with any of the conditions can result in a return to incarceration.

Being on probation means being half free. A judge can sentence you to jail or prison without a jury trial. The state does not have to prove that you are guilty beyond a reasonable doubt, only that it is more likely than not that you violated your probation. Law enforcement can search you at any time.

When you are on probation your primary goal should be to get off probation. If you strictly comply with the terms of your sentence, your probation officer can put you on non-reporting status. This will save you reporting fees and the inconvenience of reporting. It also greatly reduces the odds of you going to jail because your supervision will be far less intrusive.

Some judges will even terminate probation early when a defendant has done as instructed. This is a very happy ending. Not only does early termination restore your full liberty, it permits early dismissal of the charges against you if you were given a first offender sentence or conditional discharge.

Every probationer should take their probation very seriously. Compliance is the only thing keeping you out of jail. Report as instructed. Avoid alcohol and non-prescribed drugs. Pay your fines as soon as you possibly can. Make a list of the conditions of your probation and write a time for performing each one on your calendar. If you don't have a calendar, get one. If you aren't addicted to drugs or alcohol, can keep a schedule, and have a couple thousand dollars in your bank account or have decent credit, completing probation is no harder than getting a driver's license.

Making it through probation is much harder if you are poor. Defendants who don't have money are much more likely to have their probation revoked. Progressive attorneys often wax eloquent about how unfair this is, but these pretty words are of little use to cash-strapped probationers. If you are on probation and are struggling financially, thinking about justice is a dangerous luxury. You are going to have a far harder time getting through your probation than you would if you were affluent. Many people are working on fixing the inequities of the system and you may want to join them, but your top priority when on probation should be getting off probation.

Keep your eyes on the prize and get through probation while spending as little time in jail as possible. Courts sentence indigent defendants to pay fines and fees every day. The legislature and the appellate courts are not about to stop this. In most cases, probationers not only have to pay fines and court costs, they also must pay probation reporting fees, drug testing fees, fees for court-ordered treatment and evaluations, and restitution for court appointed attorneys. In a typical misdemeanor case, these will total $1,200 to $3,500.

Some courts let probationers "work off" their fines by performing additional community service. Community service is often credited at the rate of $10 per hour. If you can earn more than $10 an hour by working overtime or getting a second job, that is probably your best bet. However, if you can't find enough work to pay your fines, or if the only work you can find pays near the minimum wage, additional community service is a good alternative. Unfortunately, many of the fees imposed on probationers cannot be "worked off."

Probation reporting fees, drug testing fees, and court ordered counseling and treatment all must be paid for by money order. What should you do if you simply can't pay these? The short answer is do everything else you possibly can to comply with your sentence.

- Work off your fines.
- Report as directed.
- Pass every drug test.
- Go to Alcoholics Anonymous.
- Attend anger management classes
- Visit your pastor for counseling.
- Look for work.
- Most importantly, document everything you do because you may have to prove it to a judge.

The U.S. Supreme Court has held that probationers cannot be incarcerated for the inability to pay a fine. These constitutional guarantees are not always honored. Probation officers can and do seek warrants for non-payment of fees even when there is no way a probationer could have paid them.

Some trial judges routinely sentence indigent defendants to jail or prison for failure to pay. The appellate process is so slow and technical that these judges are rarely reversed on appeal. Most probationers who can't pay their fees make their situation much worse by not reporting.

When it comes to sentencing in the criminal justice system, courts have a number of different options available, including probation. Typically, courts impose probation sentences only in certain circumstances and under specific terms and conditions which must be followed by the defendant. Below is a list of some of the more common questions about probation.

Q: What is probation? Probation is the suspension of a jail sentence that allows a person convicted of a crime the chance to remain in the community instead of going to jail. Probation requires that you follow certain court-ordered rules and conditions under the supervision of a probation officer.

Typical conditions may include performing community service, meeting with your probation officer, refraining from using illegal drugs or excessive alcohol, avoiding certain people and places, and appearing in court during requested times.

Q: How long is a person "on probation"? The amount of time you are on probation depends on the offense and laws of your state. Typically, probation lasts anywhere from one to three years, but can last longer and even up to life depending on the type of conviction, such as drug or sex offenses.

Q: What are some examples of the terms or conditions of probation? A person who is placed on probation is usually required to report to a probation officer and follow a variety of conditions during the probation period. Specific conditions may include:

- Regularly meeting with your probation officer at set times;
- Appearing at any scheduled court appearances
- Paying fines or restitutions (monies to victims)
- Avoiding certain people and places
- Not traveling out of state without the permission of your probation officer
- Obeying all laws, including minor laws such as jaywalking
- Refraining from illegal drug use or excessive alcohol use
- Submitting to drug or alcohol testing.

Typically, the conditions imposed relate to the type of criminal offense. For example, a judge may require you to submit to periodic drug testing or attend a drug rehabilitation program for a drug-related offense. Similarly, a judge may require that you avoid specific people or group members for a gang-related or battery type of offense.

Q: What happens if I violate my probation? A probation violation occurs when you break any of the rules or conditions set forth in the probation order at any time during the probation period. When a potential violation is discovered, your probation officer has the discretion to simply give you a warning or can require you to attend a probation-violation hearing. If a judge determines that you violated your probation, you may face additional probation terms, heavy fines, a revoked probation, jail time, or more.

Q: What are my legal rights at a revocation hearing? During a revocation hearing, the prosecuting attorney must show that you, more likely than not, violated a term or condition of your probation using a "preponderance of the evidence" standard. Generally, you have a right to learn of any new charges against you and to present evidence in court before a neutral judge that may support your case and/or refute the evidence brought against you. You may want to consult with an attorney or other legal professional regarding the rights available to you in your particular state.

Q: What happens if my probation is revoked? A revoked probation does not automatically mean you will be sent to jail. A judge has a variety of options available during sentencing. For instance, upon a revoked probation, a judge may add an extra length to the probation, impose additional fines, or require you get counseling or attend other treatment programs. Even so, a judge may order you to serve a brief period in jail, or require you to serve the time allotted on your original sentence, depending on the circumstances. Upon conviction of probation violation, you may request a bail hearing to allow you to remain free for a brief period before having to serve time in jail or before a judge makes his or her final determination.

Q: Can I appeal a probation violation conviction? Yes. In most states, you can appeal a probation violation conviction to the state's next highest court. If the court finds that the lower court erred, or that there was insufficient evidence to support the conviction, you may have your probation violation dismissed.

Q: What's the difference between probation and parole? Probation and parole-sentencing options are similar, yet different in some ways. First, parole is a conditional release from prison that allows a prisoner to rejoin the community after serving all, or a part, of his or her prison term. Probation, on the other hand, is a sentencing order that allows a person convicted of a crime to remain out of jail altogether.

Secondly, in both cases, a person on probation or parole must follow certain court-ordered procedures and keep from getting into trouble with the law. Probation and parole violations both occur when a person either breaks the rules or fails to keep the terms of their probation or parole, including getting arrested for another offense.

Thirdly, probation and parole violations both carry significant consequences and penalties. When a probation or parole violation occurs, it may result in the person returning to jail (if on parole), or entering jail (if on probation), depending on the circumstances of the case.

Q: Can I ever shorten my time on probation? In most states, you may apply for an early release from probation, yet it is entirely discretionary (not mandatory) for a judge to allow. Typically, a deciding judge will require you to have served at least a third of your probation before eligibility for early release. In addition, a judge may require all the conditions on your probation be met, for example, rehabilitation classes completed, community service performed, and monies paid. Also, certain offenses such as DUI, sex offenses, and jail felonies are not eligible for early release in most states.

Ten Requirements for Sex Offenders Who Are on Probation

Many people agree to go on probation for sex offenses without knowing how strict the conditions of probation are for sex offenders. In many cases, it is only when they go to the probation office for their first meeting that sex offenders are told about the special conditions of probation that apply to them. By then, however, it is too late for the probationer to change his or her mind about agreeing to go on probation in the first place.

It is essential that anyone faced with the possibility of being placed on sex-offender probation understand the conditions of their probation that they will be expected to comply *before* agreeing to go on probation. Here are some of the requirements for people who are placed on sex offender probation. Ten of those requirements are:

1. A mandatory curfew from 10 p.m. to 6 a.m.

2. If the victim of the sex crime was under the age of 18 when the crime occurred, the probationer may not live within 1,000 feet of a school, day-care center, park, playground, or other place where children regularly congregate.

3. The probationer must actively participate in and successfully complete a sex-offender treatment program with qualified practitioners specifically trained to treat sex offenders at the probationer's own expense.

4. The probationer may not contact the victim of their crime either directly or indirectly unless such contact is approved by the victim, the probationer's therapist, and the sentencing judge.

5. If the victim of the crime was under the age of 18 when the crime occurred, the probationer may not have any contact with a person under the age of 18 unless certain exceptions apply.

6. If the victim of the crime was under age 18 when the crime occurred, a probationer may not work for pay or as a volunteer at any place where children regularly congregate including schools, day-care centers, parks, playgrounds, pet stores, libraries, zoos, theme parks, and malls.

7. A probationer may not view, access, own, or possess any obscene, pornographic, or sexually-stimulating visual or auditory material, including telephone, electronic media, computer programs, or computer services.

8. At least once per year, a probationer must take a polygraph examination.

9. A probationer must keep a driving log, and they are prohibited from driving a motor vehicle alone without obtaining the prior approval of their probation officer.

10. A probationer may not obtain or use a post-office box without getting the prior approval of their probation officer.

Three things that require ABSOLUTE compliance:
(Whether you are on probation or parole)

1. Keep your probation officer in "the loop." Probation officers are going to be much easier to deal with if you are on time, consistent and keep them informed. You simply can NOT over inform your probation officer. No matter what the situation is—keeping it from your probation officer is the absolute worst thing you can do. Not only will he or she be irritated about your non-disclosure, he or she could potentially violate your probation or parole and you will end up back in prison. Obviously, this is a lot easier if you are compliant with the terms of your probation, so think twice about EVERYTHING.

2. Know and follow your terms of probation. If you have questions, ask for clarification. If you aren't sure if something is allowed, ask your probation officer after reviewing your terms of probation. Saying that you "didn't know" will not excuse a violation.

3. DOCUMENT EVERYTHING. Keep a small notebook about your daily activities or record where and what you are doing on your smart phone. When a crime happens in your area—the first people the police go see is recently released offenders. If you are diligent about tracking your whereabouts and activities, you will be crossed off the list of "persons of interest" quickly.

The Dilemma of a Halfway House

Housing for ex-offenders is scarce, and if you have been placed or accepted into a halfway house, there are some things you should know. On one hand, it's better than prison...but on the other hand, halfway houses can be demanding on the patience of someone who has been recently released from prison. They are usually overcrowded and understaffed and there are every kind of person living and working in a halfway house. They can be exploitative, and there is a lot of evidence that halfway houses very often fail to provide the things you need.

That doesn't mean they can't help you and it doesn't mean that you shouldn't go to a halfway house if you have the opportunity. But like probation—your number one goal of being at the halfway house should be to get out of the halfway house and into independent living.

Most halfway houses are run by non-governmental (NGO) organizations. They are not held to a lot of standards, and many are not required to be licensed—or even trained—to provide services and support for people who have been incarcerated. They most often are run by faith-based organizations, and they will have rules and guidelines that you might not have been informed about, but you will be most certainly expected to follow.

Nearly all halfway houses will require you attend AA and/or NA meetings as well as the many different offshoots of the 12-step programs available in the area—some might even be at the halfway house itself. They may or may not allow you to have a cell phone, at least during your initial 30 days of entry. They may or may not provide you with access to healthcare. They may or may not help you—or even allow you—to further your education, get job training, or get a job. They may or may not help you with obtaining identification documents, transportation, or access to public benefits.

We have seen many of these halfway houses register you for benefits and then keep them as part of the house budget for food or other things like laundry, cleaning supplies or household items. Read anything you are given to make sure you understand what is expected of you. Don't sign any agreements without reading them carefully and don't be afraid to ask questions.

Do not expect the halfway house to provide anything other than a place to sleep at night. If they do more than that, be grateful. The standard time you can be absent from your space at the halfway house is 48 hours before you lose your bed. There are always waiting lists to get in, and they won't leave your bed available for very long.

If you use drugs or alcohol while you are in a halfway house, expect to get caught and expect to get thrown out and expect to get violated and sent back to prison. If you fail to keep your living space clean or refuse to help around the house with chores or duties, they can violate you and throw you out. It is of the upmost importance to recognize that YOU are responsible for the rest of your life. Take this opportunity seriously and get as much out of it as you can. Don't be disrespectful to the staff or other residents.

Once you are released from prison—whether it be on parole, probation, completely free to do what you want —if you are staying at a halfway house – there WILL BE a program and you WILL BE expected to participate. If you sign on to reside in a halfway house, be prepared to follow the rules. Following are 10 questions you should feel free to ask the NGO that is offering you space in their halfway house. Regardless of how you got here, it's important to make sure you have some questions answered before you get whisked away and into more trouble than perhaps you bargained for. Remember that someone is paying for you to be at the halfway house and whether it be another NGO, the State or a family member, you have the right to feel safe.

1. Is this organization legitimate?

There is nothing wrong with asking for some sort of proof that the people who are in front of you are who they say they are and they should be able to prove it. Don't be afraid to ask for identification, credentials and references – especially if you are meeting them because of being in a "crisis" situation where law enforcement is involved.

Be especially wary of Organizations who don't post contact information on their website. Any legitimate organization will have local phone numbers and an address posted on their website. Many post a phone number that is a State or National crisis hotline and you might have a great deal of trouble getting in touch with someone who is knowledgeable about the activities at a specific location.

2. Do they have any "success stories"?

There is nothing wrong with asking to hear from other people who have been in this halfway house. But don't be surprised if they either don't have anyone you can talk to or if the person they do connect you with has only recently entered themselves.

Many organizations use recently acquired residents who have not been with them very long to talk others into "joining" and they may not have experienced any actual services. Many organizations recruit former incarcerated people to assist in their recruitment efforts. They may or may not be able to help you with specific issues but be aware that they have been recruited for convincing you to choose their halfway house. A good indicator of how much help they will be is if they LISTEN to what you have to say. If they talk more than they listen – they are probably not going to be of much help as they are not likely to discover what your needs are since they are too busy talking.

Make sure you are involved in your own case plan. The boxes that they tick off on the list of program aids are sometimes designed to slow your personal growth. You will need to insist on being a part of this plan and most case managers will be pleased that you are taking initiative.

3. Are they promising to help you with legal issues?

Any organization that promises legal representation may NOT be offering you a lawyer – they may be offering you a caseworker or an advocate. A caseworker cannot represent you in court and they cannot make deals with court officials. They also may not be offering the right kind of legal representation you need. Criminal, Civil, Immigration and Family Court Cases are all very different and require a lawyer with specialized skills and experience.

Having a case worker is a GOOD thing if all you need is case management, but know the name of your case manager before you go to the halfway house, and if that person isn't there when you finally arrive, ask to speak to another case manager as quickly as possible. You will not be allowed to advance your recovery until you have agreed on a case plan with your case manager, so seeing this very important person as quickly as possible is critical to your success.

4. Do they offer residential support, and do they offer after care services?

Many organizations provide housing or "access to housing" but make sure you know exactly what kind of housing they are providing before you commit. "Access to housing" may be assistance with finding a single-family home or an apartment, but it also might be a residential group home where you will be living with other people you don't know. Adult residential facilities are not always supervised with the resident's safety in mind. They can also be tied to community-based programs and faith-based programs where the requirements are to "join".

The most common complaint we hear is when there is a promise made to "help you get you own place" but the reality is a "program" requiring you to jump through hoop after hoop to receive what you may or may not have been able to get for yourself. Be especially wary of what is commonly referred to as a "safe house".

A legitimate organization that has a proven track record of success will offer aftercare services and support for when you complete their program initiatives. Organizations that don't offer aftercare services should concern you as you are placing your life in their hands and they should accept some of the responsibility for giving you the tools you need to succeed.

5. Do they offer NON-residential support?

Should you not need or desire residential assistance or support or if you have needs that do not require a housing component, there are many resources that you may be interested in. For example – if you need legal representation and they claim to offer it – you should not have to participate in other areas of support they offer if you do not want or need them. A good organization will have no problem with you picking and choosing the services you want or need without insisting that you subscribe to ALL their services.

5. Will they respect your personal faith and/or ideology?

Your personal faith or ideology should be respected by any organization that provides support in the form of services. In fact – the subject of what you believe or don't believe shouldn't even come up if they sincerely want to help you achieve a goal. Very often – particularly with faith-based organizations – faith and ideology are the first thing they will work towards controlling. They will prioritize meetings and church services over school and work, and that is NOT going to lead you on a path to a successful life. Spirituality is an important part of your total well-being, but you should be free to determine what you define as success. Again – make sure you are a part of your own case plan. Take the initiative to progress further and faster than they anticipate.

6. How do they provide services?

Good organizations will work to help you achieve YOUR goals...not THEIR goals. They will move at your pace and they will encourage you to facilitate your own care plan. Bad organizations will insist that you participate in their path to a set of goals they set for you.

7. Is the organization sex-worker positive and are they partnering with law enforcement?

An organization is sex work/sex-worker positive when they are more concerned about WHO YOU ARE than WHAT YOU DO. They will provide you with health and safety information. This includes keeping you safe by helping you to NOT get arrested. If you need assistance of any sort and they will only help you if you cease to be a sex worker, they are NOT a sex work/sex-worker positive organization.

You will NOT be permitted to engage in sex work when staying at a halfway house and you MUST respect the rules of the house, but you should not be shamed or derided for having done so in the past. Remember – your probation or parole officer is a law enforcement officer. Following the rules of your probation or parole while you are staying at the halfway house is critical.

8. What steps do they take to protect and respect your privacy and safety?

A legitimate organization will not share your personal information with anyone without receiving written permission from you. They will not ask you to "tell your story". They will not create videos or documents that identify you as a formerly incarcerated person (present or former) or ask you to "go public" about how they assisted or supported you.

If you choose to endorse an organization and create any documents or videos or podcasts, we encourage you to create them YOURSELF, retain the copyrights to any documents, videos or podcasts and retain control of distribution. We have seen many situations where someone has agreed to speak publicly in support of an organization that provides services to at-risk populations and they continue to use the same material even after the person has returned to prison and even when the halfway house was the one who reported the violation.

Your incoming and outgoing mail should be private, but they may have rules about NOT writing to people who are still incarcerated. If this is a rule, you must follow it. If someone is sending you something valuable through the mail and you know approximately when to expect it, decide for it to be securely held until you can retrieve it personally.

Your safety and security should be very important to the organization providing housing as should your property. Theft is a common occurrence at halfway houses, and if you are not securing your valuable items, you can expect them to get stolen. Ask in advance what provisions the halfway house makes to protect your valuables.

You should also know the protocol for reporting crime or violence against you. You should know the chain of command at the halfway house and you should report inappropriate behavior to a senior staff member. If you are assaulted or any attempt is made to exploit you, you should immediately report it to a senior staff member, and if you do not feel they have sufficiently investigated you claim, you should report it to someone higher up. If you are allowed to use a common computer, make sure you log out properly when you have completed your work and do not save any passwords on a computer that everyone else uses.

Protect your identity by making sure your identification documents are safely and securely stored. Ask about the availability of lockers and locks.

9. Will they help you find paid work within three months? (Job market permitting)

You may find you need assistance finding suitable employment. You may need help with job training or school, and they should already have that in mind. Many halfway houses require a certain amount of volunteer work, but it should not supersede your paid-work opportunities. It is reasonable to require residents to participate in cleaning and upkeep of shared residential space as well as your own personal space. Pick up after yourself and be willing to commit to keeping the living environment safe and secure.

Be aware that many halfway houses volunteer their residents time at food banks, thrift stores and even soup kitchens and they receive some organizational benefits from these efforts. It is reasonable to give at least five hours a week to this kind of volunteer work – maybe more in the beginning stages of your residence when you have not found paid employment – but this should decrease as time goes on and you achieve the goals on your case plan.

10. Are they willing to provide you with written

documentation about what they are promising?

Once you and the organization agree on what they will provide – you need them to put it in writing, and the document should be dated and signed. Make sure that you are provided with a copy of the signed agreement or contract.

A word about case managers.

There are good case managers and there are not so good case managers. Sadly, there are even case managers who don't hate seeing you fail. The fact is…case managers are human beings, and they come in a variety of shapes and sizes with a very wide range of life experience and education. Most have a social work background, and they will have varying degrees of experience with incarceration.

New case managers tend to be more enthusiastic than others. Case managers that have held that position for very long time can be jaded and want to do nothing more than "check off the boxes" and go home. Case managers have a high rate of burnout. They have heard every excuse in the book, and they know a lie when they hear it. The only thing different about a lie to an experienced case manager and a newbie is that one or the other may be likely to do anything about it.

Many of our members tell us that their case manager was not available on a regular basis and never really asked for assistance in creating a case plan. If this happens to you, then use this book to create your own case plan. Use the Goal Setting portion of this workbook to create short term (30-90 days), and long-term goals (1, 3 and 5 years). As time progresses, you can change your goals to reflect lessons learned, new opportunities that may present themselves, and a change in the direction based on circumstances.

A word about the other residents.

There are going to be lot of other people in the halfway house and they are all going to be coming and going on a regular basis. The best advice we have received from other members is to KEEP TO YOURSELF and don't go looking to make these your lifelong friends. The halfway house residents are in the same situation as you are, and they have the same fears and concerns you do, but that doesn't mean you should do a lot of sharing and caring at this stage of the game. Some of our members tell us that other residents are drinking and doing drugs while they are at the halfway house and these folks will try to get you to join them. Just don't do it. Focus on yourself and your own recovery. Get your own life back. Don't try to help other residents with their personal struggles until you have a handle on your own life. By the same token, don't do anything to hurt other residents either. This is particularly a factor in housing opportunities for women. There have been a lot of reports of residents "telling on each other" to house management or staff about real or perceived wrongdoing.

Don't get involved in this kind of behavior.

Mind your own business.

Notes:

_____
_____
_____
_____
_____
_____
_____
_____
_____
_____
_____
_____
_____
_____
_____
_____
_____
_____
_____
_____
_____
_____
_____
_____
_____
_____

CHAPTER 16
Why Is Swop Behind Bars?

The Sex Workers Outreach Project (SWOP)-USA was founded in 2003 by sex workers and is "a national social justice network dedicated to the fundamental human rights of people involved in the sex trade and their communities, focusing on ending violence and stigma through education and advocacy" (SWOP-USA).

Embedded in their philosophy, which was garnered from international movements taking shape and gaining momentum during the 1970s, are sex worker rights. This sex worker rights framework acknowledges and advocates for the fundamental human rights of people involved in the sex industry and their communities. The Sex Workers Outreach Project is a US national organization that has chapters in 28 cities, and their primary goal is to end violence and stigma against sex workers through education and advocacy. SWOP USA and the affiliated chapters also fight against trafficking in the sex industry and work to educate people about the differences between consensual sex work and trafficking in the sex industry by force.

People who engage in sex work operate on a continuum between choice and coercion. Many individuals willingly and freely choose to engage in sex work, and they value their work and the privileges it affords them. There are others who may engage in sex work as a temporary endeavor or in exchange for something they need, such as housing, food, or substances. In these cases, the overarching needs create coercive conditions whereby individuals might feel as if they have no other "choice" but to engage in sex work, and therefore do so.

The criminalization of prostitution can also create coercive conditions that affect individuals who may have limited employment opportunities. For instance, being convicted of prostitution charges can severely impact one's ability to find future employment or housing, and therefore can create the conditions whereby individuals are "coerced" into engaging in illegal activities because mainstream or legal forms of employment are unavailable to them. These same conditions are exacerbated for transgender individuals, who may be denied employment based on their gender, and most especially with transgender individuals of color.

By definition, sex work requires consent. If there is no consent, then engaging in the action is trafficking. Contrary to this definition, there are individuals and organizations who propose that all prostitution be defined as trafficking in the sex industry because no one can actually consent to engage in prostitution due to its inherently exploitative nature.

Conflating sex work and trafficking in the sex industry silences those sex workers who do choose to engage in sex work, it shifts the attention and resources from actual victims of trafficking, and ultimately harms both sex workers and victims of trafficking. If all prostitution is understood to be trafficking, then no distinctions are made about the existence of force, fraud, or coercion; those aspects outlined in the Trafficking Victim Protection Act (TVPA) that define trafficking as such. Trafficking of individuals for sex requires sexual violence, coercion, or the absence of consent. And these same continuums of choice exist for individuals in manufacturing, agricultural, and domestic services, as well as others.

With more than one million women behind bars or under the control of the criminal justice system, women are the fastest growing segment of the incarcerated population, increasing at nearly double the rate of men since 1985. Expanding at 4.6% annually between 1995 and 2005, women now account for 7% of the population in state and federal prisons (ACLU).

Many women in prison have experienced physical or sexual trauma at the hands of men, and women of color are significantly overrepresented in the criminal justice system. For example, Black women represent 30% of all incarcerated women in the U.S, although they represent only 13% of the female population generally; whereas Hispanic women represent 16% of incarcerated women, and they make up only 11% of all women in the U.S

(ACLU). These numbers become even more dire when the individuals considered are transgender.

According to *Meaningful Work: Transgender Experiences in the Sex Trade*: Transgender sex workers reported high levels of interaction with the police (79.1% compared to 51.6% of non-sex worker respondents); Black and Black Multiracial sex workers reported the highest levels of interaction (87.3%) with police, and transfeminine sex workers reported higher likelihood of police interaction (83.9%) than their transmasculine counterparts (65.8%). Of these individuals, 46.8% people of color were more than twice as likely than their white counterparts (18.3%) to report being "arrested for being trans." Similarly, 58.8% of people of color and 35.2% of respondents reported being sent to jail/prison "for any reason." Black and Black Multiracial respondents had the highest rates of arrest due to their transgender status (65.3%) and being sent to jail/prison for any reason (69.6%).

The intersections between class, race, experiences of violence, gender, gender identity, stigma, discrimination, and sex work come together to create the conditions whereby a group of people are increasingly marginalized, and once criminalized for their actions, have even less opportunity to remove themselves from street economies into mainstream employment. A high percentage of women in prison claim to have experience in the commercial sex industry, and yet many individuals engaged in sexual exchanges do not self-identify as sex workers.

Approximately 60,000 people are arrested annually in the United States for prostitution and prostitution-related offenses and many are forced to participate in corrections-connected, compulsory services, either while in jail or prison or as "diversion" programs or plea bargains. These organizations often teach people involved in sex work to view themselves as victims and sex work or prostitution as inherently harmful.

SWOP Behind Bars is a chapter of the Sex Workers Outreach Project (SWOP), and our goal is to reach out to those who are disproportionately impacted by the criminalization of prostitution and other prostitution-related charges. The sex worker rights' movement has been historically represented by people in the sex industry who have greater access to privilege and power. Notably, it takes a certain amount of privilege, time, and energy to be able to organize, communicate, and work with others toward a common goal. As one of the most active organizations for sex worker rights, SWOP has been comprised primarily of white, middle-class individuals and has received critique from multiple organizations for not working to make the organization, and therefore the sex worker rights movement, more inclusive, diverse, and representative of the individuals engaging in the sex industry.

SWOP Behind Bars reaches hundreds of individuals who are currently or recently released. Our members are primarily incarcerated in prisons and live throughout the United States. Founded in 2016, our chapter is still quite young, and yet we have grown tremendously and are currently the largest SWOP chapter.

At SWOP Behind Bars, we
- Reach out to incarcerated and recently incarcerated sex workers and advocates for survivors of trafficking when they have been denied social services from both the public benefits sector and anti-trafficking groups;
- Provide newsletter, pen pals "mentoring by mail", educational materials (GED guides, substance use and abuse materials upon request, and scholarships to accredited correspondence university programs); and
- Develop alliances with faith-based communities, corrections officials, public defenders, lawyers, social service organizations, and the anti-trafficking movement.

We strive to create bridges between individuals and organizations who perhaps have different activist stances about sex work as labor or exploitation, and we work to connect with people who have similar goals in order to best engage with sex workers and victims of trafficking to best meet their needs.

Currently there are several legislative structures regarding prostitution. Prostitution can be:

1) illegal, or criminalized (as it is in the US outside of certain counties in Nevada);

2) legal and regulated (as it is in certain counties in Nevada),

3) legal to sell but not to buy (also known as "end demand" or the Nordic or Swedish models); and

4) decriminalized (all consensual sex acts are not subject to criminal charges).

Decriminalization applies to laws that criminalize adult consensual sex and related activities, including laws criminalizing sex work; buying, soliciting, or procuring; brothel-keeping and management of sex work; and vagrancy, loitering, and public nuisance that are also used to target sex workers and clients.

Decriminalization does not repeal laws against trafficking, child sexual exploitation, or other forms of violence. Evidence-based research reveals that decriminalizing prostitution decreases violence, trafficking in the sex industry, and HIV and other sexually transmitted infections.

Criminalizing prostitution not only decreases individuals' ability to seek help if trafficking were to occur (due to fear of arrest), but law enforcement practices generally increase sex workers' and trafficking victims' vulnerability to abusers' violence, promote impunity, push sex work and trafficking underground, and increase stigma and discrimination. Criminalization of prostitution can actually create the conditions whereby increased violence can be perpetuated against sex workers and victims of trafficking.

Individuals engaged in prostitution are afraid of the police and are reticent to report violence and crimes against them. Perpetrators are aware of this fear and even target sex workers because of this vulnerability. And once prosecuted for criminal charges, individuals have a more difficult time finding mainstream employment, housing, and other resources necessary to remove themselves from the incarceration and recidivism cycles.

In 2015, Amnesty International authorized their International Board to develop and adopt "a policy that supports the full decriminalization of all aspects of consensual sex work. The policy will also call on states to ensure that sex workers enjoy full and equal legal protection from exploitation, trafficking and violence" This policy draws from an extensive evidence base, including sources from UN agencies, such as the World Health Organization, UNAIDS and the UN Special Rapporteur on the Right to Health, as well as their own research conducted in four countries.

There are unique challenges for both individuals engaged in prostitution as well as victims of trafficking that correspond directly with the criminalization of prostitution:

- Arrests and detention;
- Lifelong discrimination and stigmatization;
- Lack of community and connections;

- Deportation for undocumented and documented migrants;
- Higher risk for exploitation, abuse, and violence;
- Little recourse for individuals who experience violence, discrimination and/or abuse in the workplace or home environment;
- Possible court mandated religious-based social services;
- Possible eviction and denial of future lease applications;
- A criminal record can promote discrimination and affect future employment and access to student loans, public services, and housing;
- Victims of trafficking are subjected to criminal charges; and
- Condoms are used "as evidence" of prostitution, which prevents some sex workers from carrying them and protecting themselves from sexually transmitted infections and pregnancy.

Laws prohibiting sex work are based on a moral code that does not fully consider the implications. If we are going to reform non-violent crimes like drug use and selling that are founded on societal beliefs, we also need to consider other non-violent crimes, regardless of stigma and moral objections.

The question of decriminalization or legalization cannot be limited to marijuana, but needs to be expanded to encompass sex work. We need to push for decriminalization of sex work and the correlation to decreasing crimes against women; these progressive reforms normalize and regulate sex work rather than further stigmatizing and conflating an underground industry with human trafficking.

What's Up with the Red Umbrella?

The Red Umbrella is the worldwide symbol of the sex workers' rights movement. It came into existence as the movement's symbol in 6 - 8 June 2001 in Italy during the 49th Venice Biennale of Art. Sex workers from different countries (Taiwan, Thailand, Italy, Cambodia, Germany, the USA and Austria) gathered for an event organized in part by the *Comitato per i Diritti Civili delle Prostitute from Pordenone* and marched through the streets of Venice with red umbrellas.

The so-called "World Congress of sex workers" took part in an art installation created by the Slovenian artist Tadej Pogachar. This was set up in a public area in Giardini under a tent called the "Prostitutes 'Pavilion". Activists organized video projections, exhibitions, performances, street theater, and distributed printed materials. Italian sex worker activist Pia Covre motivated the use of red umbrellas for the march: "We had to cross the city from the biennale to the Art Gallery exhibition, so we thought crossing the city with a red umbrella would make us visible. Venice is full of tourists, so we wanted to be visible from the rest of the people on the streets."

Red was chosen for its beauty and its strength, and the umbrella is meant to symbolize protection. In 2005 the International Committee on the Rights of Sex Workers in Europe adopted the red umbrella as its symbol for the rights of sex workers. Since then it has been seen increasingly around the world during events and on days like December 17, the International Day to End Violence Against Sex Workers. Later, other explanations were given. For some sex workers, red is the color of love, while others state that the umbrella symbolizes protection.

In October 2005, during the European sex workers' Brussels conference, the red umbrella was used again as a symbol. The European network the International Committee on the Rights of Sex Workers (ICRSE) finally adopted the red umbrella, and it is now used in most parts of the world.

ABOUT THE AUTHORS

Bob Pelshaw is a serial entrepreneur, consultant, speaker, Gallup-trained BP 10 Coach, formerly incarcerated citizen, and author of the award winning book and workbook *Illegal to Legal: Business Success for the (Formerly) Incarcerated* which he wrote while incarcerated. Serving time he realized many incarcerated citizens have innate business skills, often perfected on the street, that could make them into successful business owners if given tools to know how to use those skills to launch and operate a legitimate business. He is passionate about helping marginalize citizens, like himself, succeed. He and his wife live in Nebraska, but wish they lived in Florida – especially during the winter!

Jesse Maley is a sex worker and an activist and the North American Regional Representative of Network of Sex Work Projects (NSWP), a global sex worker rights organization. She is the co-founder of SWOP Behind Bars, one of the leaders of the SWOP Orlando Chapter and is on the board of directors of SWOP-USA. She was incarcerated numerous times for prostitution and prostitution- related charges and is dedicated to bringing unity to the sex worker rights movement as well as being committed to the full decriminalization of sex work worldwide. She is married and lives in Florida.

Jill McCracken, PhD is an Associate Professor of Rhetoric at the University of South Florida St. Petersburg. She is also a Co-Founder/Co-Director of SWOP Behind Bars, and one of the leaders of SWOP Tampa Bay chapter. Having worked with sex workers and victims of trafficking for over fourteen years, Jill has expanded her research to include women who have been, or currently are incarcerated. Her primary areas of research focus on sex work and trafficking in the sex industry, the impact of sexuality education on marginalized communities, and incarcerated women. Drawing on ethnographic and qualitative research methods, Jill increasingly integrates community-based, participatory research in her work with these specific populations. She provides training on harm reduction, sex work and trafficking in the sex industry, and sexuality education. She lives in Florida with her son.

ACKNOWLEDGMENTS

SWOP Behind Bars would like to thank our beautiful and vibrant community of sex workers and allies for their constant support of our work. We couldn't do it without you! We especially appreciate the support of SWOPUSA National for their early support of our fledgling chapter and for all the hard work you put in in the earliest of days of activism that allowed us to flourish.

We would like to specifically mention Maggie, Matisse, Savannah, Ceyenne, Melanie, Bella, John M and Katherine. We would to thank Bob Pelshaw for assisting us in the publication and distribution of this workbook.

A special thanks to Joe A. at Seminole County Jail for allowing us early education about the complications of reaching incarcerated populations and heartfelt appreciation for the anti-trafficking movement in Central Florida for their deliberate and intentional efforts to throw us under the bus. Without that shove, we would never have discovered our true purpose.

Thank you to Amber B and Kamyla for enduring the horrific and public humiliations that sparked the desire to launch a specific program for incarcerated sex workers.

We are forever in your debt.

Made in the USA
Columbia, SC
17 November 2020

24735792R00104